CU00950212

6
7

104

267

CONTENTS

48
ALL THE GOALS

76
WHAT THEY SAID

78
ALL THE GOALS

114
THE LAST WORD

TOTTENHAM HOTSPUR FOOTBALL AND ATHLETIC CO. LTD, REG. OFFICE: LILYWHITE HOUSE, 782 HIGH ROAD, LONDON, N17 0BX

Chairman: Daniel Levy
Operations and Finance Director: Matthew Collecott
Executive Director: Donna-Maria Cullen
Director of Football Administration and Governance: Rebecca Caplehorn
Chief Commercial Officer: Todd Kline
Managing Director, Football: Fabio Paratici
Non-Executive Director: Jonathan Turner
Performance Director: Grètar Steinsson

Head Coach: Antonio Conte
Assistant Head Coach: Cristian Stellini
First Team Coach: Ryan Mason
Technical and Analytics Coach: Gianluca Conte
First Team Goalkeeper Coach: Marco Savorani
Fitness Coaches: Costantino Coratti, Stefano Bruno, Gian Piero Ventrone (1960-2022)
Set Pieces Coach: Gianni Vio

OFFICIAL PUBLICATION:
Head of Publications: Jon Rayner
Contributor: Andy Greeves
Head of Creative & Brand: Kieran Murphy
Design Lead: Mark Jones
Senior Artworker: Nick Allen
Graphic Designer: Peter Burt

REACH SPORT:
Managing Director: Steve Hanrahan
Senior Executive Art Editor: Rick Cooke
Executive Editor: Paul Dove
Senior Production Journalist: Simon Monk
Designer: Adam Ward
Senior Writer: Chris Brereton
Commercial Director: Will Beedles
Marketing & Communications Manager: Claire Brown

Photography:
Getty Images, THFC, PA Photos, Mirrorpix

Printed by
Micropress

Published by

Reach Sport

THE GOAL STATISTIC

49
SCORED WITH
HEAD

2
SCORED WITH
OTHER
(BODY PART)

GOALS BY SEASON

2011/12	1
2013/14	4
2014/15	31
2015/16	28
2016/17	35
2017/18	41
2018/19	24
2019/20	24
2020/21	33
2021/22	27
2022/23	19

165
SCORED WITH
RIGHT FOOT

51
SCORED WITH
LEFT FOOT

GOALS BY VENUE

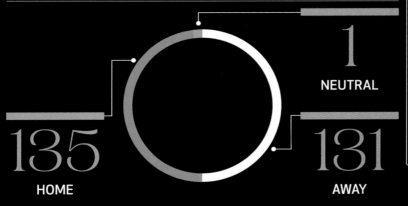

1 NEUTRAL

135 HOME

131 AWAY

GOALS BY AREA

236 SCORED IN THE BOX

39 PENALTIES

31 SCORED OUTSIDE THE BOX

1 DIRECT FREE-KICKS

GOALS BY TIME

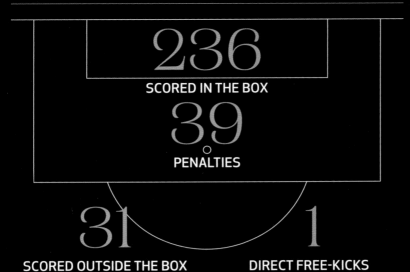

1-15 MINS	16-30 MINS	31-45 MINS	46-60 MINS	61-75 MINS	76-90 MINS	EXTRA TIME
35	42	42	51	45	51	1

GOALS BY TEAMS

Team	Goals
Leicester City	19
Everton	15
Arsenal	14
West Ham United	11
Southampton	11
Stoke City	10
Crystal Palace	10
Burnley	9
Brighton & Hove Albion	9
West Bromwich Albion	9
Newcastle United	9
Liverpool	8
Fulham	8
Aston Villa	7
Chelsea	7
Bournemouth	7
Norwich City	6
Manchester City	5
Manchester United	5
Hull City	5
Wolverhampton Wanderers	5
Asteras Tripolis	4
Huddersfield Town	4
Borussia Dortmund	4
NS Mura	4
Swansea City	3
Sunderland	3
PSV	3
Maccabi Haifa	3
Olympiakos	3
Nottingham Forest	3
APOEL Nicosia	3
Watford	3
Leeds United	3
AFC Wimbledon	2
AEL Limassol	2
Dinamo Zagreb	2
Queens Park Rangers	2
Sheffield United	2
Paços de Ferreira	2
Crvena Zvezda	2
Barcelona	1
FK Qarabag	1
Lokomotiv Plovdiv	1
Morecambe	1
Brentford	1
Monaco	1
Juventus	1
Shkendija	1
Shamrock Rovers	1
Tranmere Rovers	1
RSC Anderlecht	1
Newport County	1
Rochdale	1
Bayern Munich	1
Eintracht Frankfurt	1
Portsmouth	1
Middlesbrough	1
Cardiff City	1
Ludogorets Razgrad	1
Besiktas	1
CSKA Moscow	1

CHASING GLORY

OUR NEW RECORD GOALSCORER **HARRY KANE** REFLECTS ON HIS JOURNEY SO FAR AND EXPLAINS HOW HE'S STILL GOT PLENTY OF TARGETS FOR THE FUTURE, DESPITE SECURING HIS PLACE IN THE SPURS HISTORY BOOKS FOREVER

Growing up, I always thought I'd love to be Tottenham Hotspur's all-time goalscorer, although I never really gave it too much attention once I started playing. Even when I was 100 goals away or so, it just wasn't something that I was focussed on because records and accolades are great but, in football, there is always another game around the corner to occupy your mind.

"I take a great deal of pride in the fact that the work I have put in throughout my career has taken me to this point."

Now that it's happened though, I can say that it's an incredible personal achievement for me and to overtake a player of the calibre of Jimmy Greaves, one of the greatest forwards the game has ever seen, is something of which I am extremely proud. I was able to enjoy the moment at the time, however football never stops. There is the next game to play, the next record to break and for me now, it's just about setting my own standards to see how many goals I can score, to see where that takes me and us as a club.

I also take a great deal of pride in the fact that the work I have put in throughout my career has taken me to this point. To become a professional footballer takes a lot of resilience, hard

work and patience and you have to be ready for the opportunity when it comes.

I think back to when I first joined Spurs at the age of 11, I didn't really know much about nutrition or sports science. As I got to about 15 or 16, that's when it became a real part of my learning curve in terms of being a professional. I also had a growth spurt around that time and physically, I was able to do a lot more above my age group.

There were times as a youngster when I probably thought I was ready for the Tottenham first team but actually, I still had a lot of developing to do, mentally and physically. At that age, you are so eager to get into the team, to play in the Premier League and to play for England, you just want to jump straight to the top. You have to be patient though and, while I was to a certain degree, I learnt that patience is so important.

My loan spells – at Leyton Orient, Millwall, Norwich City and Leicester City – played a huge part in my development. They were key for many reasons and perhaps the main one was it made me realise how important football was. When you're playing Academy football, it's all about learning and developing, whereas when I went on loan, people are playing for their jobs, for their families and it really opened my eyes.

Also, you're playing in front of fans, there is pressure in the games and, of course, it's physical! So, as a young boy going out on loan at the age of 17 to Leyton Orient in League One, it was a great experience. At Millwall too, I really enjoyed it. Kenny Jackett was a great manager for me. We were in a tough relegation battle at the time but Kenny believed in me and that gave me a

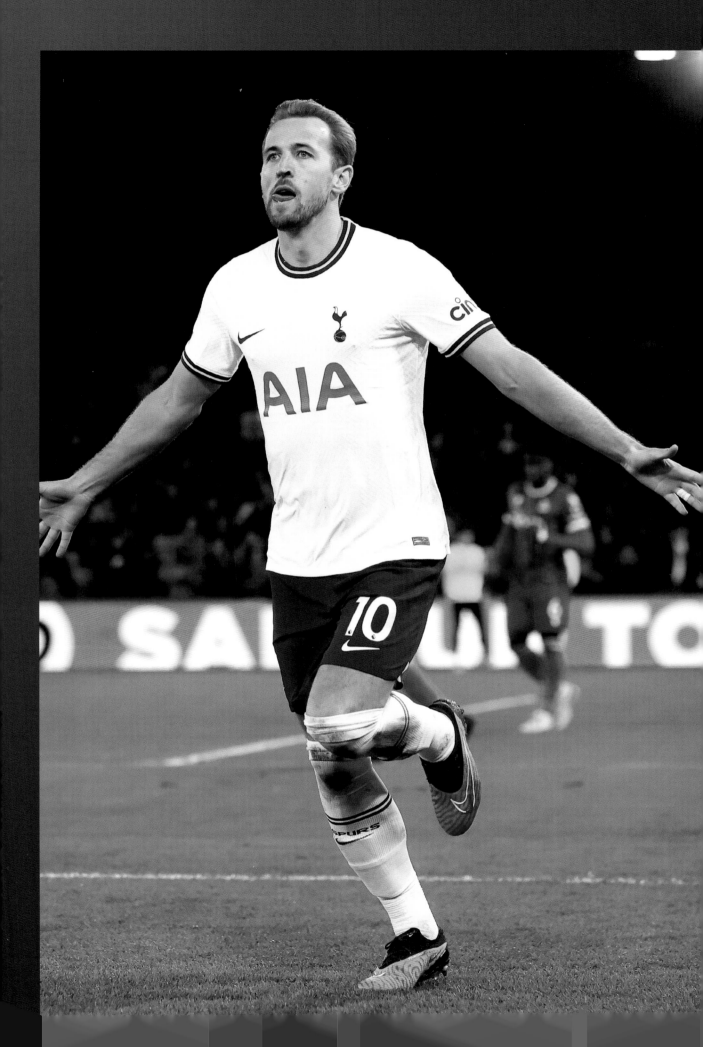

THE '100 CLUB' - OUR ALL-TIME RECORD GOALSCORERS

1 - HARRY KANE - 2011-present
- 267 goals in 416 appearances

2 - JIMMY GREAVES - 1961-70
- 266/379

3 - BOBBY SMITH - 1955-64
- 208/317

4 - MARTIN CHIVERS - 1968-76
- 174/367

5 - CLIFF JONES - 1958-68
- 159/378

6 - JERMAIN DEFOE - 2004-2014
- 143/363

7 - HEUNG-MIN SON - 2015-present
- 139/353

8 - GEORGE HUNT - 1930-37
- 138/198

9 - LEN DUQUEMIN - 1947-57
- 134/307

10 - ALAN GILZEAN - 1964-74
- 133/439

11 - TEDDY SHERINGHAM - 1992-2003
- 124/277

12 - ROBBIE KEANE - 2002-2011
- 122/306

13 - LES BENNETT - 1946-54
- 117/294

14 - JIMMY DIMMOCK - 1919-31
- 112/438

15 - GLENN HODDLE - 1975-87
- 110/490

16 - BERT BLISS - 1912-22
- 104/215

17= BILLY MINTER - 1908-19
- 101/263

17= JOHNNY MORRISON - 1933-39
- 101/154

Records from joining the Football League in 1908/09. Up to and including 5 February 2023

real confidence boost. I scored seven goals and we stayed up. All of my loans helped define me and gave me the mentality to go on and achieve what I have done at Spurs. Consistency and mentality are my two biggest strengths. I think the game now is so difficult, we come up against such good players week in, week out, physically strong players so you need to be consistent and mentally strong to cope with that.

When I was younger, my aim was to always be consistent. Anyone can maybe have one season where they score a lot of goals, but can they do it year on year? That's something I

"It's an incredible personal achievement for me and to overtake a player of the calibre of Jimmy Greaves, one of the greatest forwards the game has ever seen, is something of which I am extremely proud."

have been fortunate enough to do and I'm really proud of that.

So, what would I say is a classic Harry Kane goal? For me, it would probably be from the right-hand side of the goal, hitting it back across the goalkeeper and low into the bottom corner. That's something I've done throughout my whole career, even back in my Academy days – that's my go-to finish!

There are so many people who have helped me throughout my career to date and enabled me to become Tottenham Hotspur's all-time record goalscorer that it would be impossible for me to thank them all individually. However, I'd like to take this opportunity to thank my wife Kate, my family and friends, my team-mates both past and present, everyone at the Club, from top to bottom – who have helped me along the way – and, of course, all the fans who have supported me on every step of my journey. From the bottom of my heart, I thank you all.

Looking ahead, there is still a lot I want to achieve. People will look at me and my career for goals and goal records however, for sure, I would love to add trophies to that. I still feel like I have plenty of years left to achieve that so, in terms of my final legacy, we'll have to wait and see…

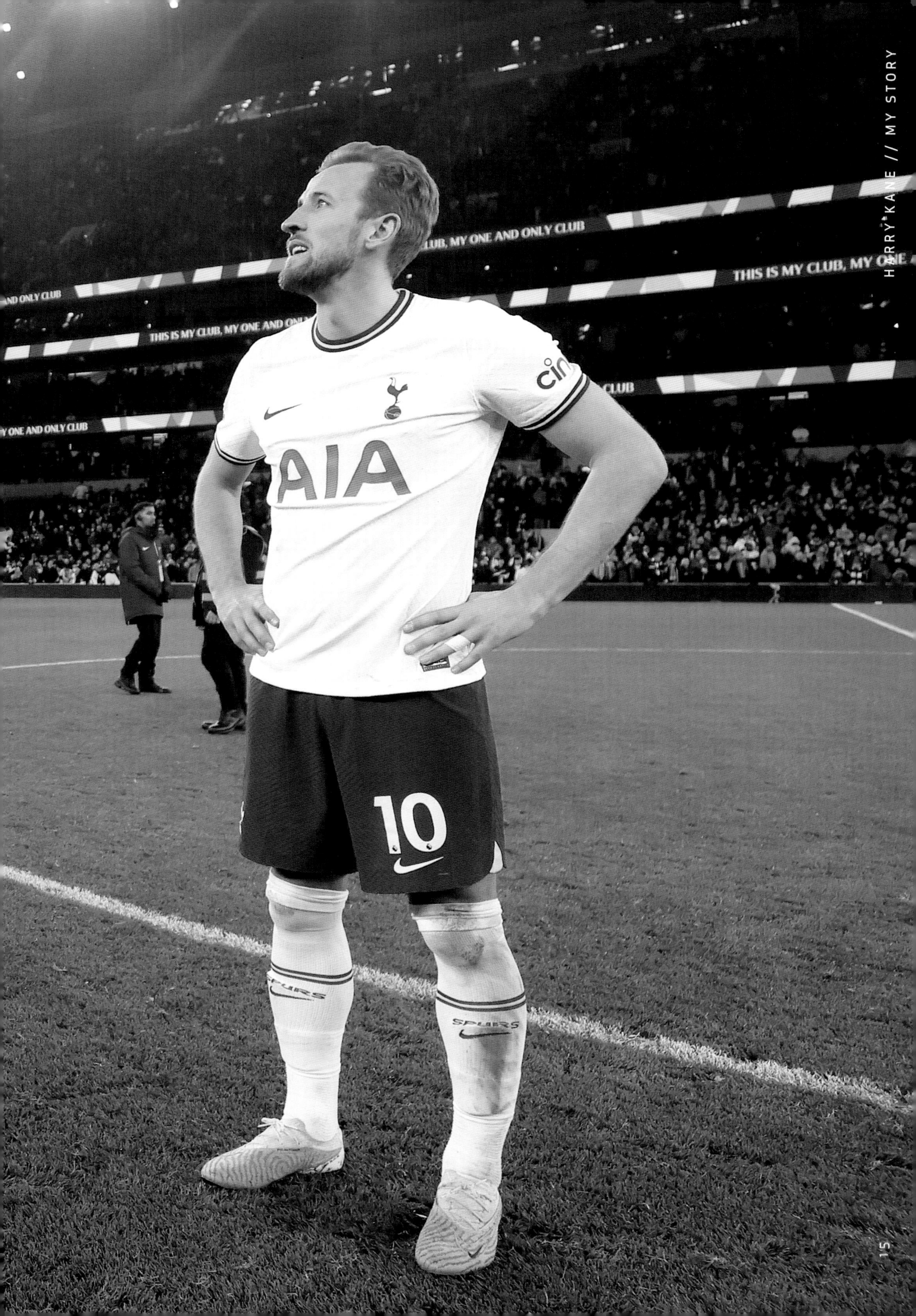
THIS IS MY CLUB, MY ONE AND ONLY CLUB
AIA
10
SPURS

1

v Shamrock Rovers A (EL) - 15/12/11
90+1, right foot shot, inside area, W 4-0

On a cold December night in 2011, in the unfamiliar surroundings of Tallaght Stadium – the Dublin-based home of Shamrock Rovers – Tottenham Hotspur's number 37, Harry Kane, opened his goalscoring account for the Club. By this stage, his journey had taken him through the Spurs Academy, where his hard work and desire to succeed had made him a standout player in our youth teams, and earned him a loan move to Leyton Orient for the second half of the 2010/11 campaign. That's where he scored his first senior goal, in a 4-0 win over Sheffield Wednesday at Brisbane Road, and he netted five times in 18 appearances for the O's. His Spurs debut duly followed at the start of the following season, featuring in a Europa League play-off, second leg against Hearts at White Hart Lane after we'd won the first game 5-0. He could have scored his first Spurs goal that night but missed a penalty, something that would become a rarity as his career progressed.

Instead, goal number one came in the group stage of that Europa League campaign, a few months later. On the face of it, there was nothing too spectacular about the goal. It came in the 91st minute, the last one in our 4-0 win in a game which turned out to be immaterial as results elsewhere saw us knocked out of the competition. But watch it again and you'll see all the attributes that has made Kane an elite striker – movement as Danny Rose delivers a cross from the left, anticipation as Andros Townsend nods the ball back into the danger zone, and technique to swivel and fire home right-footed from the edge of the six-yard box. Perhaps still raw qualities back then, but they were there for all to see – and goal number one was in the bag. No-one could have foreseen how many more were going to follow though…

COMPETITIONS KEY

PL – Premier League
FAC – FA Cup
LC – League Cup
CL – Champions League
EL – Europa League
ECL – Europa Conference League

2

v Hull City H (LC) - 30/10/13
108, left foot shot, outside area,
W 10-9 on pens

Almost two years later – after loan spells at Millwall, Norwich City and Leicester City, which yielded a further 11 goals – Harry was back at Spurs and quickly back among the goals. Trailing 2-1 in extra time to Hull City in the Carabao Cup, he drilled left-footed into the far corner from just outside the area to draw us level, his first White Hart Lane goal.

3

v Sunderland H (PL) - 7/4/14
59, right foot shot, inside area, W 5-1

A goal in Europe, a goal in the League Cup – and now his first Premier League strike. Sunderland were the N17 visitors and, with the score at 1-1, Kane showed his striking instincts to touch home Christian Eriksen's teasing cross to put us ahead in the 59th minute in front of the North Stand and pave the way for a 5-1 win.

4

v West Bromwich Albion A (PL) - 12/4/14
70, header, inside area, D 3-3

Five days later at The Hawthorns, Aaron Lennon dug out a cross from the right and Kane was there to head home from six yards out past Ben Foster for his second Premier League goal, as we came from 0-3 down to draw with West Bromwich Albion.

5

v Fulham H (PL) - 19/4/14
48, header, inside area, W 3-1

Another right-wing cross from Lennon, albeit with his left foot this time, and another headed goal from Kane, who outmuscled Johnny Heitinga to glance home a 48th-minute header at the Paxton Road end of White Hart Lane and put us ahead in the contest.

v AEL A (EL) - 21/8/14
80, right foot shot, inside area, W 2-1

The 2014/15 campaign will always be remembered as Harry's breakthrough season and he got the ball rolling in a Europa League fixture in Cyprus. We'd trailed to AEL but Roberto Soldado levelled in the 74th minute before Kane – now wearing the number 18 shirt – latched onto an Erik Lamela pass and rifled into the roof of the net to score his first goal under new manager Mauricio Pochettino.

v AEL H (EL) - 28/8/14
45, right foot shot, edge of the box, W 3-0

A week later, Harry scored another against the Cypriots from Limassol in the White Hart Lane return. Receiving a pass from Paulinho, he steadied himself before sliding the ball home from 18 yards out to give us the lead on the stroke of half-time.

v Nottingham Forest H (LC) - 24/9/14
90+1, right foot shot, inside area, W 3-1

v Besiktas H (EL) - 2/10/14
27, left foot shot, outside area, D 1-1

On the night when his good mate and fellow Academy graduate Ryan Mason scored his first Spurs goal, Harry continued his good form with a fine finish to wrap up this Capital One Cup tie. Lamela was the creator with a smart throughball to release Kane behind the Forest defence and he finished unerringly into the bottom corner from the inside right channel.

A first goal from distance from Harry, who picked up possession from Nabil Bentaleb, turned his marker and strode forwards before arrowing a left-footed drive from 25 yards out into the bottom corner of the Besiktas net in the group stage encounter.

10

v Asteras Tripolis H (EL) - 23/10/14
13, right foot shot, outside area, W 5-1

11

v Asteras Tripolis H (EL) - 23/10/14
75, right foot shot, inside area, W 5-1

12

v Asteras Tripolis H (EL) - 23/10/14
81, header, inside area, W 5-1

One of the more eventful games of Kane's Spurs career, as he scored his first-ever professional hat-trick but ended the night wearing the goalkeepers' jersey – and that wasn't even the biggest talking point of the evening! That accolade went to Erik Lamela, whose 'rabona' style goal against the Greek side was a moment of outstanding and outrageous skill.

But back to Harry, who reached double figures for Spurs with his first of the night which opened the scoring. It was another from distance, this time off his right foot as he powered home past Asteras goalkeeper Tomas Kosicky in the 13th minute.

After a brace from Lamela, Kane added his second and our fourth with 15 minutes remaining, snaffling up the rebound to turn the ball home after Kosicky had spilled Mousa Dembele's effort. And his first treble was completed on 81 minutes, heading home unmarked at the back post from Federico Fazio's cross.

That wasn't the end of Harry's drama though as he donned the goalkeeping gloves in the final minutes following a red card for Hugo Lloris and having used all three substitutes. Unfortunately, his ability between the sticks wasn't as good as his ability to score goals, allowing a late free-kick to slip through his hands for a consolation goal for the visitors!

13

v Brighton & Hove Albion
H (LC) - 29/10/14
74, right foot shot, inside area, W 2-0

A real poacher's goal to secure a Capital One Cup win over Brighton at the Lane. Kane started the move out on the left, finding Andros Townsend whose cross was prodded goalwards by Soldado. Goalkeeper Christian Walton kept it out but the ball ran loose inside the area and Kane – who had continued his run into the area – reacted quickest, beating Aaron Hughes to the ball to slam home our second on the night.

14

v Aston Villa A (PL) - 2/11/14
90, right foot shot, outside area, W 2-1

There are few more significant goals in Harry Kane's Spurs career than this one against Aston Villa. At the time, the forward was featuring – and scoring - regularly in cup competitions but was having to settle for a place on the bench when it came to the Premier League. It all changed after this game. We trailed to an Andreas Weimann goal but were given an opportunity when Christian Benteke was sent off on 65 minutes, shortly after Kane had been introduced as a substitute.

His energy and enthusiasm helped to tire the Villa side and our dominance finally paid off when Nacer Chadli equalised with six minutes left. Then, as the game entered its final minutes, Carlos Sanchez upended Townsend 25 yards from goal and Kane grabbed the ball for the resulting free-kick. He hit a right-foot shot which flicked off the head of Nathan Baker and nestled in the back of the net, sparking wild celebrations from Kane and his team-mates in front of our delighted away fans.

For Harry, that was effectively the moment his career took off. Selected to start our next Premier League game against Stoke City, he's basically been in our team ever since and, if Kane's on the pitch, the goals have duly followed.

15

v Asteras Tripolis A (EL) - 6/11/14
42, header, inside area, W 2-0

Harry reached double figures for the season when he headed home our second goal in this Europa League win. Three minutes before the break Andros Townsend delivered a teasing cross and Kane was on hand to plant a header past 'keeper Tomas Kosicky.

16

v Hull City A (PL) - 23/11/14
61, left foot shot, inside area, W 2-1

Harry made it nine goals in 10 games in this away victory. When Christian Eriksen's free-kick came back off the post, Harry pounced instantly to fire home a 61st-minute equaliser. Eriksen bagged the second as we came from behind to take all three points.

17

v Swansea City A (PL) - 14/12/14
4, header, inside area, W 2-1

There were just four minutes on the clock when Harry opened the scoring. Christian Eriksen sent a corner deep into the Swans' penalty area where Kane rose highest to send a bullet-like header past goalkeeper Gerhard Tremmel.

18

v Newcastle United H (LC) - 17/12/14
65, left foot shot, inside area, W 4-0

With Spurs already two goals to the good in this Capital One Cup tie, Kane latched on to a clever through ball and blasted home a fierce low left-foot shot after 63 minutes which realistically ended the tie as a contest.

19

v Burnley H (PL) - 20/12/14
21, header, inside area, W 2-1

Kane opened the scoring on 21 minutes, timing his run perfectly to meet Nacer Chadli's left-wing cross and head home at the near post in a victory which edged us above Arsenal in the table.

20

v Leicester City A (PL) - 26/12/14
1, left foot shot, inside area, W 2-1

A first-minute opener from Harry this time. In similar fashion to his goal in the previous match, Nacer Chadli was again the provider from the left as Kane nipped ahead of Foxes' defender Wes Morgan and sent a left-foot effort past Ben Hamer.

MY TOP 5

21

v Chelsea H (PL) - 1/1/15
30, right foot shot, outside area, W 5-3

It proved a perfect start to 2015 at White Hart Lane as Harry scored his first Premier League brace in a thrilling 5-3 London derby victory over league leaders Chelsea on New Year's Day. Harry's first goal of the afternoon arrived on 30 minutes as he levelled the match at 1-1 when he cut in from the left, held off several challenges and fired a powerful low right-foot shot past Thibaut Courtois from outside the area.

Kane put us well on course for three points in the second half with a turn and shot inside the area which made the score 4-1 after he neatly rolled Nemanja Matic before dispatching a smart shot that nestled inside the far post.

"This was a big one for me. To get Man of the Match, score two goals, two assists against a team who would be Premier League champions, that settled it in my head that I could do it against any opponent, any team. That gave me all the self-belief I needed."

——————————————————————————————— **HARRY KANE**

22

v Chelsea H (PL) - 1/1/15
52, right foot shot, inside area, W 5-3

23

v Crystal Palace A (PL) - 10/1/15
49, right foot shot, edge of area, L 2-1

Four minutes into the second half at
Selhurst Park, Kane intelligently and calmly
shuffled for space before scoring with a
low right-foot effort from the edge of the
penalty area that flew into the bottom
corner. That goal gave Spurs the lead but
the home side struck back to win 2-1.

24

v West Bromwich Albion A (PL) - 31/1/15
15, right foot shot, inside area, W 3-0

Kane's first goal arrived after 15 minutes and doubled our lead following Christian Eriksen's sixth-minute opener. Mousa Dembele surged forward, laid the ball into Harry's path and, inside the area, he swiftly cut back on to his right foot and dispatched an unstoppable driven effort.

He added his second from penalty spot after Albion defender Joleon Lescott had handled Kyle Waker's cross and Harry made no mistake from 12 yards.

25

v West Bromwich Albion A (PL) - 31/1/15
64, penalty, W 3-0

MY TOP 5

"I think this was the moment the fans fell in love with me. You score two goals in a north London derby to win 2-1 at White Hart Lane and people will never forget that. The fans could see the passion in my eyes, the celebrations. We had a special connection after that goal."

— HARRY KANE

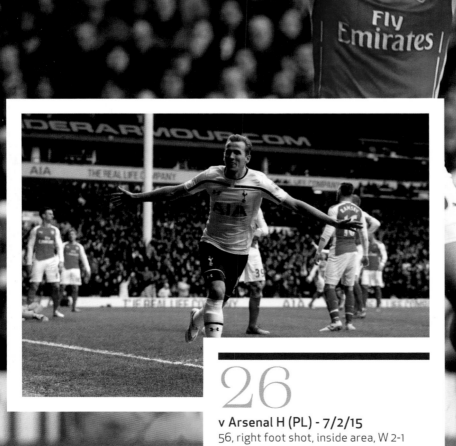

26

v Arsenal H (PL) - 7/2/15
56, right foot shot, inside area, W 2-1

27

v Arsenal H (PL) - 7/2/15
86, header, inside area, W 2-1

Harry's second-half brace saw us come from behind at the break to win a memorable north London derby. Eleven minutes after the break, he bagged his first goal against our big rivals to level the match, pouncing at the back post to crash home a loose ball after Mousa Dembele's flicked header from a corner had been partially cleared. Four minutes from time White Hart Lane erupted with delight as Kane rose to powerfully head home in front of the North Stand for a sensational winner.

28

v Liverpool A (PL) - 10/2/15
26, right foot shot, inside area, L 2-3

Kane marked his first visit to Anfield with a goal as Spurs were narrowly beaten in a five-goal thriller. After 26 minutes, he was played in by Erik Lamela and, with time and space afforded to him, he fired home a right-foot shot from 10 yards to make it 1-1.

29

v West Ham United H (PL) - 22/2/15
90+6, right foot shot, inside area, D 2-2

Trailing 2-1, we were awarded an injury-time penalty and up stepped Kane only to be denied by Hammers' goalkeeper Adrian who dived to his right and repelled the spot-kick. But Harry instinctively smashed home the rebound to make it 2-2.

30

v Queens Park Rangers A (PL) - 7/3/15
34, header, inside area, W 2-1

Harry's first goal in this 2-1 win came when Andros Townsend's free-kick was floated towards the back post area, Rangers 'keeper Rob Green came out to punch clear but Kane arrived first to head into an unguarded net. Then, on 68 minutes, he collected a long ball forward from Ryan Mason before confidently rounding Green and slotting home a left-foot effort in front of the travelling fans.

31

v Queens Park Rangers A (PL) - 7/3/15
68, left foot shot, inside area, W 2-1

32
v Leicester City H (PL) - 21/3/15
6, left foot shot, inside area, W 4-3

34
v Leicester City H (PL) - 21/3/15
64, penalty, W 4-3

33
v Leicester City H (PL) - 21/3/15
13, left foot shot, inside area, W 4-3

A first Premier League hat-trick came soon after his first senior England call-up in 4-3 win over Leicester City. Just six minutes in, a corner was flicked on at the near post by the boot of Eric Dier, Foxes goalkeeper Kasper Schmeichel could only palm the ball into the path of Kane, who slotted home from close range. He added his second with a left-foot strike from inside the area and, after David Nugent upended Danny Rose in the area, Harry rifled home the resulting penalty to complete his first Premier League treble after 64 minutes.

35

v Newcastle United A (PL) - 19/4/15
90+1, right foot shot, inside area, W 3-1

Having marked his England debut with a goal, Harry was back in the groove at club level at St James' Park. He netted our final goal in injury time when he finished off a counter-attacking move by sending a smart right-foot shot past Tim Krul from inside the hosts' penalty area.

36

v Everton A (PL) - 24/5/15
24, header, inside area, W 1-0

Kane capped off an outstanding 2014/15 with his 31st goal of the campaign in the final Premier League game of the season. There were 24 minutes on the clock when Harry ghosted between two Everton defenders to meet Eric Dier's deep cross and plant his header past Tim Howard.

37

v Manchester City H (PL) - 26/9/15
61, right foot shot, inside area, W 4-1

Harry opened his Spurs scoring account for 2015/16 when he netted the third goal in this fine win against Manchester City. When Christian Eriksen's free-kick came back off the woodwork on 61 minutes Kane was alive, alert and on hand to stab a right foot shot into an empty net.

38 v Bournemouth A (PL) - 24/10/15
9, penalty, W 5-1

39 v Bournemouth A (PL) - 24/10/15
56, right foot shot, inside area, W 5-1

40 v Bournemouth A (PL) - 24/10/15
63, right foot shot, inside area, W 5-1

A first Premier League hat-trick away from the Lane came at Bournemouth. Harry got our equaliser on nine minutes when he converted a penalty past Artur Boruc, while his second, and Spurs' fourth, came after 56 minutes when he peeled away from his marker at the far post and guided home Christian Eriksen's cross with a clever right-foot finish. On 63 minutes – as Boruc spilt a headed effort on goal – Harry simply hammered the loose ball home from two yards out to complete another treble.

41 v Aston Villa H (PL) - 31/10/15
90+3, right foot shot, inside area, W 3-1

Leading 2-1 in added time, Harry made the points safe when he crashed home our third goal. Erik Lamela picked out Kane in the penalty area and he instinctively sent a first-time shot curling past Villa 'keeper Brad Guzan and into the roof of the net.

42 v Anderlecht H (EL) - 5/11/15
29, right foot shot, outside area, W 2-1

Harry set Spurs on their way to a Europa League victory after 29 minutes when he latched on to a superb reverse pass from Christian Eriksen and instantly dispatched a missile-like effort from the edge of the area that flew into the bottom corner.

43

v Arsenal A (PL) - 7/11/15
32, right foot shot, inside area, D 1-1

After bagging a brace against the Gunners at White Hart Lane in his previous North London derby, Harry scored his first goal on enemy territory to put us one up at the Emirates Stadium. Danny Rose played a ball inside the channel and Kane nipped in front of Per Mertesacker before applying a composed finish 13 minutes before the break.

44

v West Ham United H (PL) - 21/11/15
23, left foot shot, inside area, W 4-1

Kane's opening goal was a ruthless close-range left-foot finish after 23 minutes and followed a sharp turn after the ball had fallen at his feet from Dele Alli's deflected long-range shot. His second arrived five minutes after the interval when he struck a right-foot effort from just outside the area. This latest double helped Spurs equal a club record by going 12 Premier League games unbeaten.

45

v West Ham United H (PL) - 21/11/15
50, right foot shot, outside area, W 4-1

46

v Qarabag A (EL) - 26/11/15
78, header, inside area, W 1-0

Harry scored the only goal of the game in this victory that secured our place in the Europa League last 32. On 78 minutes, Heung-Min Son flicked on a Christian Eriksen corner and Harry was able to head home from a yard for his ninth goal in six games.

47

v Southampton A (PL) - 19/12/15
40, right foot shot, inside area, W 2-0

Showing power, pace and a cool head in front of goal, Harry gave us the lead at Southampton. Collecting a loose ball, Kane ran towards the Saints goal, holding off a number of challenges before beating Paulo Gazzaniga with a clinical finish.

48

v Norwich City H (PL) - 26/12/15
26, penalty, W 3-0

49

v Norwich City H (PL) - 26/12/15
42, right foot shot, inside area, W 3-0

Another two goals on Boxing Day! Kane won the penalty he scored on 26 minutes, making a positive run into the Canaries 18-yard-box before being upended by Declan Rudd. Three minutes before the break, he made it 2-0 as he powered a right-footed shot from a narrow angle inside the penalty area into the bottom corner.

50

v Leicester City H (FAC) - 10/1/16
89, penalty, D 2-2

Harry scored a late penalty in this FA Cup third round draw to ensure a replay at the King Power Stadium. We were awarded a spot-kick after the Foxes' Nathan Dyer had handled in the area and Kane dispatched his penalty in style, to bring up his half century of Spurs goals.

51

v Sunderland H (PL) - 16/1/16
79, penalty, W 4-1

With Spurs leading 3-1 at the time, Black Cats debutant Jan Kirchhoff fouled Danny Rose and referee Mike Dean pointed to the spot. An emphatic penalty from Kane saw him beat future England team-mate Jordan Pickford.

52

Crystal Palace A (PL) - 23/1/16
63, header, inside area, W 3-1

On a day best remembered for Dele Alli's virtuoso goal, it was Harry who brought us level in our eventual victory at Crystal Palace. Kane showed real desire to get to a Nacer Chadli cross, towering above defender Damien Delaney to head home.

53

v Norwich City A (PL) - 2/2/16
30, penalty, W 3-0

Kane's second brace against Norwich City during the 2015/16 season, scoring in both halves after Dele Alli had given us the lead. He converted a penalty on the half-hour mark, sending Declan Rudd the wrong way with his spot-kick, before showing great composure for his second goal on 90 minutes, beating Rudd with a well-placed left-foot shot.

54

v Norwich City A (PL) - 2/2/16
90, left foot shot, inside area, W 3-0

55

Manchester City A (PL) - 14/2/16
53, penalty, W 2-1

Harry's 53rd-minute penalty helped us to a huge win at the Etihad Stadium. His spot-kick, which came after Raheem Sterling was adjudged to have handled inside his 18-yard-box by referee Mark Clattenburg, went to goalkeeper Joe Hart's left.

MY TOP 5

"Toby Alderweireld had just scored to make it 1-1 and everyone was off their seats already and two minutes or so later I curled that in. That was the loudest I ever heard White Hart Lane so to be the one that made that happen is so special. It's one of the best feelings I've ever had scoring a goal, that moment still gives me goosebumps now."

HARRY KANE

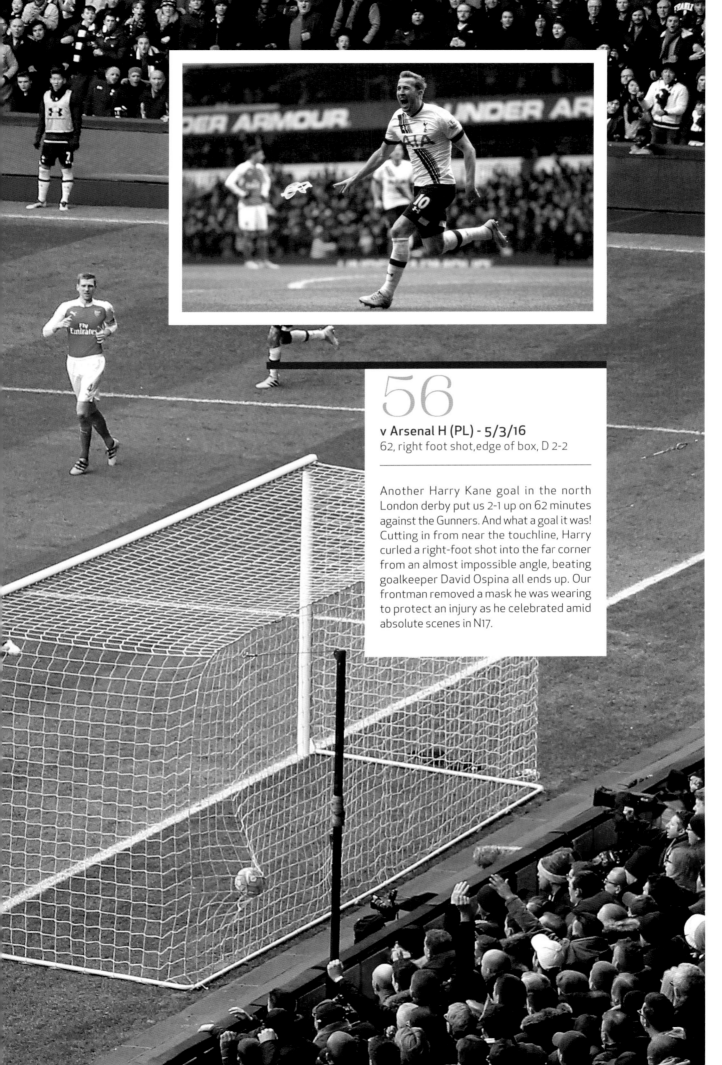

56

v Arsenal H (PL) - 5/3/16
62, right foot shot,edge of box, D 2-2

Another Harry Kane goal in the north London derby put us 2-1 up on 62 minutes against the Gunners. And what a goal it was! Cutting in from near the touchline, Harry curled a right-foot shot into the far corner from an almost impossible angle, beating goalkeeper David Ospina all ends up. Our frontman removed a mask he was wearing to protect an injury as he celebrated amid absolute scenes in N17.

57
v Aston Villa A (PL) - 13/3/16
45, left foot shot, inside area, W 2-0

58
v Aston Villa A (PL) - 13/3/16
48, right foot shot, inside area, W 2-0

Two-goal Kane secured three points with strikes either side of the half-time interval. Latching onto Dele Alli's quickly taken free-kick, Harry fired across goalkeeper Brad Guzan just before the break. Three minutes into the second period, Dele was the supplier once again as Harry prodded home a right-foot shot.

59
v Bournemouth H (PL) - 20/3/16
1, right foot shot, inside area, W 3-0

60
v Bournemouth H (PL) - 20/3/16
16, left foot shot, inside area, W 3-0

An instinctive finish from Kane put us 1-0 up against the Cherries after just 43 seconds. Kyle Walker played a low cross into the penalty area and Harry slid in to beat Simon Francis to the ball and arrow a shot across Artur Boruc into the back of the net. His second of the day on 16 minutes was a real treat as Dele Alli weighted a precise through ball and Kane's finish into the bottom corner was equally inch-perfect.

61
Liverpool A (PL) - 2/4/16
63, right foot shot, inside area, D 1-1

Harry produced a striking masterclass to draw us level in a Premier League clash at Anfield. Collecting a ball from Christian Eriksen inside the Reds area, near enough with his back to goal, he was able to turn marker Dejan Lovren before setting himself and sending a right-footed shot into the bottom corner.

62
v Stoke City A (PL) - 18/4/16
9, right foot shot, inside area, W 4-0

63
v Stoke City A (PL) - 18/4/16
71, right foot shot, inside area, W 4-0

An outstanding team display saw us score four without reply, with Harry central to all that was good about Spurs on the night. He put us in front on nine minutes with a sublime, curling effort from just inside the penalty area. And Erik Lamela and Kane sprung Stoke's offside trap on 71 minutes, with the Argentine rolling the ball across for our number 10 to bag his brace from close-range.

64
v Chelsea A (PL) - 2/5/16
35, left foot shot, inside area, D 2-2

Still in the race for the Premier League title as we faced Chelsea, Harry gave us the perfect start at Stamford Bridge. Needing a win to remain in the title chase, Kane collected a pass from Erik Lamela before going on to round Asmir Begovic in the Blues goal to put us one up. While the night ended in disappointment with a 2-2 draw, Kane's 25th league strike of the season saw him bag the Premier League Golden Boot.

65

v Stoke City A (PL) - 10/9/16
70, left foot shot, inside area, W 4-0

A 50th Premier League goal for Harry was also his first club strike of the 2016/17 season. It was one of his easiest goals in our colours too, as Heung-Min Son's cross fizzed across the Potters six-yard-box and Harry took a touch before hammering a left-footed shot home from a few yards out.

66

Sunderland H (PL) - 18/9/16
59, right foot shot, inside area, W 1-0

Harry scored the only goal of the game in our victory over the Black Cats at White Hart Lane. After 14 second-half minutes, Kyle Walker swung a free-kick into the visitors' penalty area which was headed across the six-yard-box by Dele Alli, giving Kane the simple task of rifling home from close range.

67

v Arsenal A (PL) - 6/11/16
51, penalty, D 1-1

Kane scored in another north London derby as he converted a second-half penalty at the Emirates. Shortly after the half-time interval, Mousa Dembele was fouled in the Gunners 18-yard-box by Laurent Koscielny and Harry levelled with a right-footed spot-kick.

68

v West Ham United H (PL) - 19/11/16
89, left foot shot, inside area, W 3-2

Two late goals to give Spurs a dramatic victory over the Hammers! Trailing 2-1 with just a minute of the 90 remaining, Harry met Heung-Min Son's cross and turned home from close range to level the score. Two minutes later, Son was brought down in the West Ham penalty area and Harry made no mistake with a powerful, confident spot-kick to maintain our unbeaten start to the Premier League campaign.

69

v West Ham United H (PL) - 19/11/16
90+1, penalty, W 3-2

70

v Monaco A (CL) - 22/11/16
52, penalty, L 2-1

Another expertly-taken penalty on 52 minutes levelled the score in our Champions League match at Stade Louis II. Harry's spot-kick was cancelled out just 38 seconds later though as the home side regained the lead.

THE ORIGINAL GOAL MACHINE

WHILE **HARRY KANE'S** NAME WILL NOW SIT IN THE BOOKS AS OUR RECORD GOALSCORER, THE MAN HE REPLACED WILL ALWAYS BE REMEMBERED AS ONE OF TOTTENHAM HOTSPUR'S GREATEST-EVER PLAYERS

By Jon Rayner

"**Do you think I'll break your record, Jimmy?**"
"No chance," quipped Greavsie, quick as a flash. It was a brief but wonderfully touching conversation as Harry Kane and Jimmy Greaves – the two greatest goalscorers in the long history of Tottenham Hotspur – met for the only time.

The poignant occasion occurred at Hotspur Way in October 2017, when Jimmy was invited to our Training Centre to meet Harry and the team. Although confined to a wheelchair at the time having suffered a severe stroke two-and-a-half years earlier, Jimmy showed he'd lost none of his Cockney wit and charm when the pair discussed the club's goalscoring record.

Back then of course, it belonged to Greavsie, whose tally of 266 Spurs goals had stood for almost 50 years. Harry was still a long way off, although he had just fired in 35 goals in 2016/17 and netted his 100th goal in our colours the previous month. Jimmy knew though, that if anyone was going to take his mantle of Tottenham's all-time goalscorer, it was likely to be Kane and you got the feeling that he was more than happy with that.

And, perhaps inspired by meeting a player regarded by many as the finest goalscorer English football has ever seen, Harry crashed home another two goals in our 4-1 defeat of Liverpool at Wembley just two days later to move up to 112.

Fast forward to February 2023 and the record that many had considered impossible to surpass was finally broken as Harry slotted home a crucial winner against Manchester CIty.

As well as their prodigious goalscoring abilities, there are a few similarities between Greaves and Kane. Born within just a few miles of each other in east London – albeit 53 years apart – they were both born into football-loving families and were kicking balls in their back gardens as soon as they could walk. But their paths to goalscoring stardom were quite different.

Jimmy was always regarded as a natural scorer, someone simply born to score goals and that he certainly did. His first-ever organised game came at the age of 10 for his school side – Southwood Lane Junior School – when he played inside right and scored twice. A goal on his debut would be a familiar trait throughout his career.

There was never any doubt that Harry would become a top player, but he had to work hard to make it to the very pinnacle of the sport. He clearly had ability as a youngster, however he wasn't one that stood out during his early teenage years. But Harry knew what was needed to progress. Determined, committed and dedicated to achieving his own targets, he knuckled down and put in the hard graft, reaping the rewards for those efforts by becoming one of the greatest strikers of his generation.

"I DON'T KNOW WHY, BUT I FOUND IT EASY. SCORING GOALS CAME NATURALLY TO ME"

While Greavsie never played anywhere other than in the forward line, Harry spent time as an attacking midfielder during his formative years in youth football before bulking up, growing stronger and becoming more physically built for the number nine position. That experience of playing both positions went a long way to making him the player he is today, someone who can create as well as score, who can link the play and provide a killer pass just as well as he can find the back of the net.

For Jimmy though, it was all about the goals. "I don't know why, but I found it easy. Scoring goals came naturally to me," he once said. As his reputation as a hugely gifted young footballer started to spread, all the London clubs craved his signature as a schoolboy, but it was Chelsea who won the race. During the 1956/57 season, Greavsie scored a staggering 122 goals for the Blues in the South East Counties League and signed a professional contract in May 1957.

Three months later, aged just 17, he made his league debut for Chelsea – coincidentally against Spurs at White Hart Lane. He scored, of course, in a 1-1 draw. Over the course of the next four years, Jimmy netted 124 league goals in 157 games for the Stamford Bridge side, finishing as the top scorer in Division One in 1958/59 and 1960/61. A brief sojourn to Italy followed when he

joined AC Milan in June 1961 but, although he scored nine goals in 14 matches, it wasn't an enjoyable spell.

Just six months later, Greavsie was back in London and it was Bill Nicholson that brought him 'home'. His Spurs side had just swept all before them by winning the League and FA Cup Double in 1960/61 and what better way to strengthen the team than by signing the ultimate goalscoring machine. Jimmy started in style, scoring a hat-trick on his Tottenham debut which included a spectacular scissor-kick as we beat Blackpool – and so began the love affair between Jimmy and Spurs that continues to thrive today, even in the great man's absence.

His arrival definitely improved an already great team. Jimmy played a huge part in helping us retain the FA Cup in 1962 and make history in 1963 when we won the European Cup Winners' Cup, the first English side to win a European trophy. Naturally he scored in both finals.

Greavsie's goals just simply never stopped flowing. In his first full season at White Hart Lane in 1962/63, he scored 37 league goals which remains a club record and, after topping the First Division scoring charts in 1964/65, he became the first player to do so in three consecutive seasons. More silverware followed in 1967 when we won the FA Cup again, beating his former side Chelsea at Wembley.

It was on 10 January 1970 that Jimmy scored his 266th and final Spurs goal – fittingly at the Lane in a 2-1 win over Derby County. It's a number that has appeared in our record books for over 50 years, one that is etched in the minds of Spurs fans everywhere, who instantly know how many goals Greavsie scored in lilywhite.

Now it's been surpassed, replaced by a new number – yet to be determined as Harry continues to add to his tally. What Kane's final figure will be remains to be seen, but one thing is for sure – Jimmy Greaves' 266 goals tell another story that will never be forgotten.

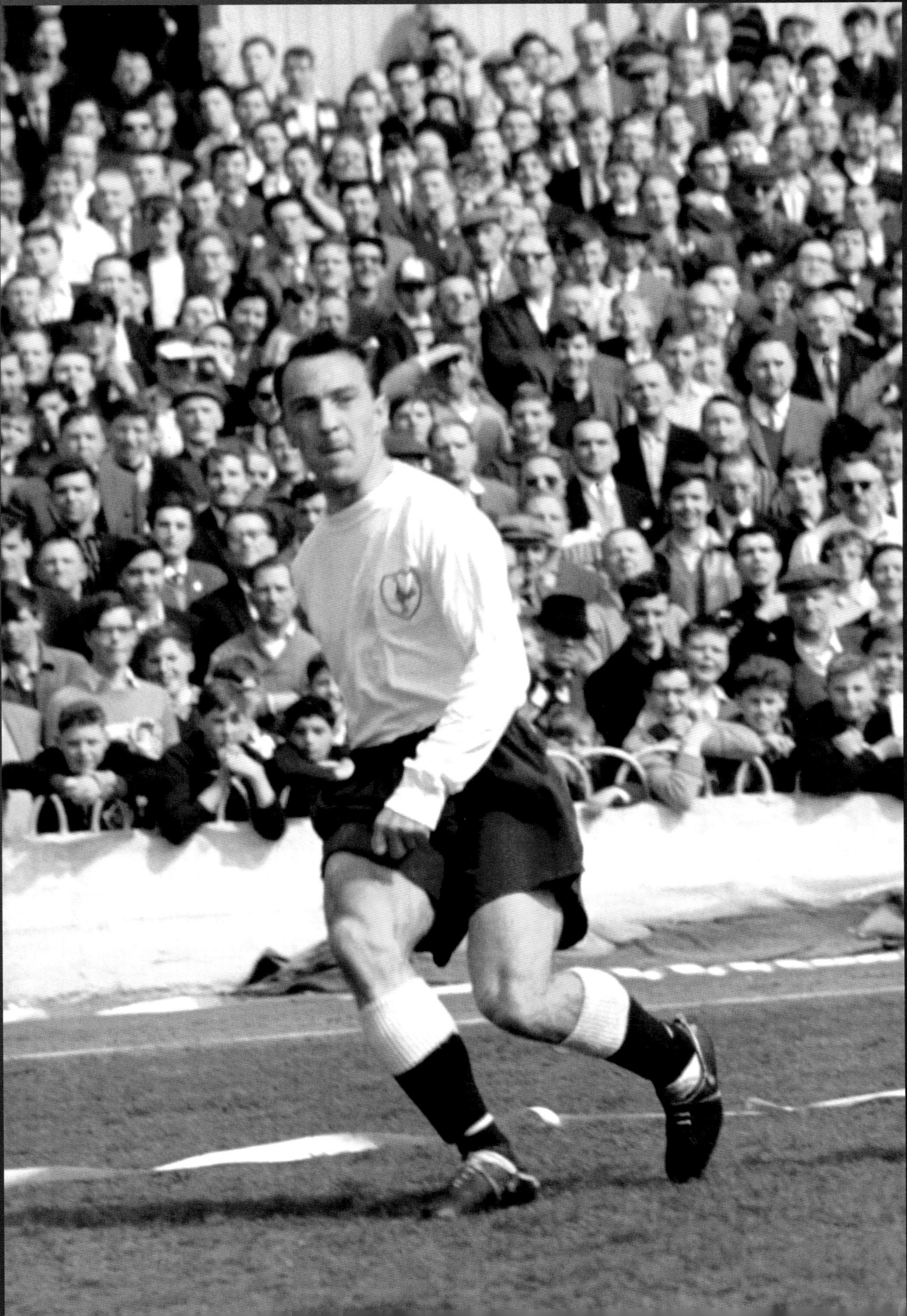

71
v Swansea City H (PL) - 03/12/16
39, penalty, W 5-0

72
v Swansea City H (PL) - 03/12/16
49, right foot shot, inside area, W 5-0

Harry scored the opener in this thrashing of Swansea City from the penalty spot on 39 minutes, before adding his second with a powerful low shot from Heung-Min Son's unintentional lay-off. Kane thought he'd secured a hat-trick just after the hour mark, but his 'goal' was flagged for offside.

73
v CSKA H (CL) - 7/12/16
45+1, right foot shot, inside area, W 3-1

74
v Southampton A (PL) - 28/12/16
52, header, inside area, W 4-1

A win at Wembley saw us confirm a third-place finish in our Champions League group and progress to the Europa League knockout stage. Kane put us 2-1 up when he tapped in from a Danny Rose cross.

Harry ended his run of three league games without scoring when he headed in from a Christian Eriksen corner early in the second half to make it 2-1 at Southampton in our last match of 2016.

75
v Watford A (PL) - 1/1/17
27, right foot shot, inside area, W 4-1

76
v Watford A (PL) - 1/1/17
33, right foot shot, inside area, W 4-1

Kane's habit of scoring on New Year's Day continued as he got onto the end of a delightful Kieran Trippier cross to put Spurs ahead just before the half-hour mark. Trippier was provider once again five minutes later when his perfectly weighted pass found Harry who lifted the ball over our former 'keeper Heurelho Gomes in the Watford goal.

77

v West Bromwich Albion H (PL) - 14/1/17
12, right foot shot, inside area, W4-0

Just days after becoming a dad for the first time, Harry scored his fourth hat-trick for Spurs. We dominated from the start and a lovely through ball from Christian Eriksen provided Kane with his first goal after just 12 minutes. He was on target again in the second half with a fine volley from Kyle Walker's cross to make it 3-0, before firing home from a Dele Alli scooped pass on 82 minutes. The victory saw us equal our club record of six straight Premier League wins.

78

v West Bromwich Albion H (PL) - 14/1/17
77, right foot shot, inside area, W4-0

79

v West Bromwich Albion H (PL) - 14/1/17
82, right foot shot, inside area, W4-0

80

v Middlesbrough H (PL) - 4/2/17
58, penalty, W1-0

Our winning streak continued with a 1-0 victory over Middlesbrough. Harry was on target from the penalty spot once again in the second half, following Bernardo Espinosa's foul on Heung-Min Son.

81

v Fulham A (FAC) - 19/2/17
16, left foot shot, inside area, W 3-0

Kane hit his second hat-trick of 2017 as we beat Championship outfit Fulham 3-0 to reach the FA Cup quarter-finals. He gave Spurs the lead early on when he finished from close range after a Christian Eriksen cross. Five minutes into the second half, the Denmark international picked out Kane again, who slotted the ball through Marcus Bettinelli's legs in the Whites goal before completing his treble with a coolly taken strike on 73 minutes.

82

v Fulham A (FAC) - 19/2/17
51, right foot shot, inside area, W 3-0

83

v Fulham A (FAC) - 19/2/17
73, right foot shot, inside area, W 3-0

84

v Stoke City H (PL) - 26/2/17
14, right foot shot, inside area, W 4-0

Another week and another treble – this time in the league. Harry struck three times within the space of 23 first-half minutes before assisting Dele Alli for Spurs' fourth. The striker's first goal – which he fired low into the net – was also the 100th of his club career. Harry doubled our lead just after the half-hour mark with a fantastic half-volley from a Christian Eriksen corner. Five minutes later Kane was on target again when Eriksen tapped a free-kick into the striker's path and his deflected strike beat Stoke keeper Lee Grant.

85
v Stoke City H (PL) - 26/2/17
32, left foot shot, outside area, W 4-0

86
v Stoke City H (PL) - 26/2/17
37, right foot shot, outside area, W 4-0

87

v Everton H (PL) - 5/3/17
20, right foot shot, outside area, W3-2

A brace from Harry helped Spurs to a 3-2 victory over Everton. He opened his account in the 20th minute with a thumping strike from 25 yards and doubled our advantage 10 minutes into the second half, picking up a pass from Dele Alli and side-footing the ball into the Toffees' goal.

88

v Everton H (PL) - 5/3/17
56, right foot shot, inside area, W3-2

89

v Bournemouth H (PL) - 15/4/17
48, left foot shot, inside area, W4-0

Three minutes into the second half, Kane showed his strength to shrug off the Cherries defence and shoot low into the corner for our third goal, and his 20th of the season. The strike saw him became just the fourth player to score 20 Premier League goals in three consecutive seasons.

90

v Chelsea (FAC) - 22/4/17
18, header, inside area, L 4-2

Harry's diving, glancing header from a Christian Eriksen cross saw us draw level with London rivals Chelsea in the 18th minute of our FA Cup semi-final. It wasn't our day though, as the Blues progressed.

91

v Arsenal H (PL) - 30/4/17
58, penalty, W 2-0

We put our FA Cup disappointment firmly behind us with this victory and oh, how Harry loves to score against Arsenal! The match was decided with two goals in three second-half minutes as Dele Alli finished from close range before Kane put away a confident spot-kick after he'd been brought down by Gabriel. The result confirmed we would finish above our local rivals for the first time since 1995.

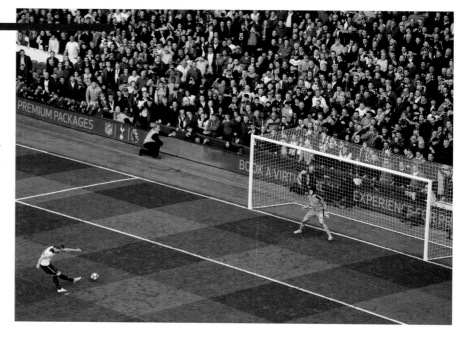

92

v Manchester United H (PL) - 14/5/17
48, right foot shot, inside area, W 2-1

Fittingly, it was Harry who scored our last goal at White Hart Lane as we bid a fond farewell to our home of the previous 118 years. He flicked his right foot at a Christian Eriksen free-kick to beat David De Gea from close-range to put us 2-0 up early in the second half after Victor Wanyama had given us an early lead on an emotional afternoon in N17.

93

v Leicester City A (PL) - 19/5/17
25, right foot shot, inside area, W 6-1

94

v Leicester City A (PL) - 19/5/17
63, header, inside area, W 6-1

Harry ran riot at the King Power Stadium netting four of Spurs' six goals – his first quadruple in our colours. His first on 25 minutes was a right footed shot from the centre of the box into the bottom left corner of the hosts' net and, shortly after the hour mark, a header from close range made it 3-1. With the Premier League Golden Boot award within touching distance, Harry smashed home two 20-yard strikes in the dying minutes of the game to take his scoring tally to 26 for the season with one match left to play.

95

v Leicester City A (PL) - 19/5/17
89, right foot shot, outside area, W 6-1

96

v Leicester City A (PL) - 19/5/17
90, right foot shot, edge of box, W 6-1

97
v Hull City A (PL) - 21/5/17
11, left foot shot, outside area, W7-1

Kane secured his second successive Golden Boot with a goalscoring masterclass at Hull. It took the striker just 11 minutes to break the deadlock as he fired home from the edge of the box. Two minutes later he was on target again, tapping in from a Kieran Trippier cross.

He completed his eighth hat-trick for Spurs – his fourth of the 2016/17 campaign – with a confident finish after being played in by Dele, taking his final Premier League tally to 29.

98
v Hull City A (PL) - 21/5/17
13, left foot shot, inside area, W 7-1

99
v Hull City A (PL) - 21/5/17
72, left foot shot, inside area, W 7-1

100

v Everton A (PL) - 9/9/17
28, right foot shot, outside area, W 3-0

Harry's 100th goal in our colours may have been unintentional, but it still counts!

The striker admits luck was involved when his cross-shot from the right looped over Toffees 'keeper Jordan Pickford and found the net for his Spurs century. After Christian Eriksen scored our second, Kane neatly finished from a Ben Davies cross to make it 3-0 early in the second half.

101

v Everton A (PL) - 9/9/17
46, left foot shot, inside area, W 3-0

MY TOP 5

102

v Borussia Dortmund H (CL) - 13/9/17
15, left foot shot, inside area, W 3-1

Another brace from Harry helped get our Champions League campaign off to a positive start at Wembley Stadium. With the score at 1-1, Kane put us back in front in the 15th minute with a left-footed effort after beating a couple of defenders and his second of the evening was a low shot inside the far post on the hour mark to make it 3-1.

"I loved my first goal against Dortmund at Wembley as it was a bit different. I picked up the ball around the halfway line, got through one player and ran through to finish, that was a different type of goal for me and one that I really enjoyed."

HARRY KANE

103

v Borussia Dortmund H (CL) - 13/9/17
60, left foot shot, inside area, W 3-1

104
v West Ham United A (PL)
- 23/9/17
34, header, inside area, W 3-2

105
v West Ham United A (PL)
- 23/9/17
38, left foot shot, inside area, W 3-2

Kane made no mistake with a leaping header from a Dele Alli cross for our opener against the Hammers and added his second just minutes later, this time a simple tap in after goalkeeper Joe Hart blocked an initial effort from Dele. Christian Eriksen added a third, but we had to survive a late West Ham fightback to win.

106

v APOEL A (CL) - 26/9/17
39, left foot shot, inside area, W 3-0

Harry's first Champions League hat-trick saw us brush aside APOEL. He picked up a lovely pass from Toby Alderweireld to slot the ball into the bottom left corner for the first, then doubled our lead just after the hour mark with a cool, right-footed finish from the edge of the penalty area after a Moussa Sissoko cross. Kane completed his treble five minutes later with a confident header.

107
v APOEL A (CL) - 26/9/17
62, right foot shot, inside area, W 3-0

108
v APOEL A (CL) - 26/9/17
67, header, inside area, W 3-0

109

v Huddersfield Town A (PL) - 30/9/17

9, right foot shot, inside area, W 4-0

110

v Huddersfield Town A (PL) - 30/9/17

23, left foot shot, outside area, W 4-0

Spurs maintained their perfect away record at the start of the 2017/18 Premier League season with this victory. Two quality strikes from Harry saw his goal tally for September rise to 13. His first of the afternoon came from a Kieran Trippier header and he raced into the box to calmly slot the ball home, before making it 3-0 midway through the first half with a sweet curling shot into the top left corner.

111

v Liverpool H (PL) - 22/10/17

4, left foot shot, inside area, W 4-1

112

v Liverpool H (PL) - 22/10/17

56, right foot shot, inside area, W 4-1

Harry scored the first of his two goals after just four minutes as Spurs put on a spectacular display to beat Liverpool. Kieran Trippier chipped a pass over the Reds defence and Kane took the ball round goalkeeper Simon Mignolet to finish from 12 yards and was then in the right place to score our fourth of the afternoon after the Reds failed to clear a free-kick.

113

v Borussia Dortmund A (CL) - 21/11/17
49, right foot shot, inside area, W 2-1

Another Champions League goal, creating space for himself to shoot from the edge of the box to equalise against Dortmund on 49 minutes. Heung-Min Son confirmed our victory to maintain our unbeaten run in Europe.

114
v West Bromwich Albion H (PL) - 25/11/17
74, left foot shot, inside area, D 1-1

Harry tapped home from close range after a Dele Alli cross to rescue a point at Wembley. We dominated possession, but failed to make many clear-cut chances until Harry hit the target on 74 minutes.

115
v Leicester City A (PL) - 28/11/17
79, right foot shot, inside area, L 2-1

On target once more for his 10th goal of the season, but his late close-range effort at the King Power Stadium proved to be only a consolation, with the hosts going 2-0 up before the break.

116
v Stoke City H (PL) - 11/12/17
54, header, inside area, W 5-0

117
v Stoke City H (PL) - 11/12/17
65, left foot shot, outside area, W 5-0

Two more goals against Stoke City to round off a comfortable afternoon. We were 2-0 up when Harry's first came from a deep cross from our left flank from Ben Davies, the striker rising above Erik Pieters to head home at the far post. Then, Heung-Min Son laid the ball into Harry's path and he finished first time with a fine, left-footed effort from just outside the Potters' penalty area.

118
v Burnley A (PL) - 23/12/17
7, penalty, W 3-0

120
v Burnley A (PL) - 23/12/17
79, left foot shot, inside area, W 3-0

119
v Burnley A (PL) - 23/12/17
69, right foot shot, inside area, W 3-0

Two days before Christmas, Harry enjoyed an early present as he bagged a hat-trick – his 10th in our colours – which also saw him equal Alan Shearer's record of 36 Premier League goals in a calendar year. He opened the scoring with an excellent penalty kick on seven minutes, before making it two on 69 minutes as he raced on to Moussa Sissoko's through-ball and produced a calm right-footed finish. He wrapped up the win with a powerful left-footed effort into the bottom corner on 79 minutes.

121

v Southampton H (PL) - 26/12/17

22, header, inside area, W 5-2

122

v Southampton H (PL) - 26/12/17

39, left foot shot, inside area, W 5-2

123

v Southampton H (PL) - 26/12/17

67, left foot shot, inside area, W 5-2

Harry's opener saw him break the Premier League record for the number of goals scored in a calendar year. He headed home his 37th league goal in 12 months on 22 minutes to beat Alan Shearer's previous record of 36, which was set in 1995.

Our number 10 added two further goals to his tally that afternoon too, with a left foot shot from inside the area on 39 minutes before completing his 11th Spurs hat-trick with a close-range finish shortly after the hour mark.

124

**v AFC Wimbledon H
(FAC) - 7/1/18**
63, right foot shot, inside area, W 3-0

125

**v AFC Wimbledon H
(FAC) - 7/1/18**
65, left foot shot, inside area, W 3-0

A quick-fire brace from Kane saw him bundle the ball into the net from close range on 62 minutes after Moussa Sissoko had delivered from the right. Just two minutes later, Kyle Walker-Peters' shot was deflected to Harry in the box who finished with his left foot.

126

v Everton H (PL) - 13/1/18
47, right foot shot, inside area, W 4-0

Harry became Spurs' all-time Premier League goalscorer with two close-range finishes either side of the break. Heung-Min Son had opened the scoring at Wembley Stadium before providing the pass for Harry's first of the afternoon. His second, just after the hour mark, saw him get onto the end of an Eric Dier cross to tap the ball home to take his Premier League goal tally to 98, one more than Teddy Sheringham scored for the Club.

127

v Everton H (PL) - 13/1/18
59, left foot shot, inside area, W 4-0

128
v Southampton A (PL) - 21/1/18
18, header, inside area, D 1-1

Kane headed home from a Ben Davies corner on 18 minutes, just three minutes after the home side had taken the lead, to give Spurs a share of the spoils at St Mary's.

129
v Newport County A (FAC) - 28/1/18
82, right foot shot, inside area, D 1-1

Our number 10 came to the rescue once again as he scored a late goal to keep us in the FA Cup. League Two side Newport took the lead in the first half of the fourth-round tie, but Kane forced a replay when he tapped in at the back post from a corner.

130
v Liverpool A (PL) - 4/2/18
90+5, penalty, D 2-2

Kane equalised with the last kick of the game during a dramatic encounter at Anfield. Mo Salah's stoppage-time goal looked to have given the hosts the victory but the referee awarded a penalty with seconds left after Virgil van Dijk brought down Erik Lamela, and Harry slammed home the spot-kick.

131
v Arsenal H (PL) - 10/2/18
49, header, inside area, W 1-0

A towering header from Harry secured all three points in the north London derby. He rose above Laurent Koscielny to direct home Ben Davies' cross shortly after the restart to make it seven goals in seven league games against Arsenal for the England striker.

132
v Juventus A (CL) - 13/2/18
35, left foot shot, inside area, D 2-2

After going 2-0 down within nine minutes, Kane launched our comeback as he latched on to Dele Alli's pass and rounded Juventus 'keeper Gianluigi Buffon to find the back of the net on 35 minutes.

133
v Rochdale A (FAC) - 18/2/18
88, penalty, D 2-2

Harry's late penalty put Spurs 2-1 up on his 200th appearance for the Club. The striker rifled the ball into the bottom corner after Dele Alli was fouled in the area.

134
v Crystal Palace A (PL) - 25/2/18
88, header, inside area, W 1-0

Kane's header on 88 minutes proved the matchwinner at Palace. He peeled away at the back post to guide in Christian Eriksen's corner for his 35th goal of the season in all competitions.

135
v Stoke City A (PL) - 7/4/18
63, header, inside area, W 2-1

Spurs' winner at Stoke was initially awarded to Christian Eriksen but the Premier League's goals accreditation panel later gave it to Harry, confirming he had the final touch on the ball from the Dane's teasing free-kick.

136
v Brighton & Hove Albion A (PL) - 17/4/18
48, right foot shot, inside area, D 1-1

We took the lead at Brighton with Harry's 26th league goal of the campaign. Heung-Min Son kept the ball in play at the byline before laying it back to Harry who fired home from close range.

137
v Watford H (PL) - 30/4/18
48, right foot shot, inside area, W 2-0

Harry doubled our lead early in the second period when he converted Kieran Trippier's pass with a right-foot finish from the edge of the six-yard box.

138
v Newcastle United H (PL) - 9/5/18
50, right foot shot, inside area, W 1-0

Kane scored the only goal as we beat Newcastle to confirm Champions League qualification for a third successive season. Heung-Min Son set up Harry in the area who curled the ball into the top corner.

139

v Leicester City H (PL) - 13/5/18
7, left foot shot, inside area, W 5-4

140

v Leicester City H (PL) - 13/5/18
76, right foot shot, inside area, W 5-4

Harry scored twice in a nine-goal thriller at Wembley. His first goal, a low hard drive after seven minutes, drew us level with the Foxes after Jamie Vardy's early opener. And Kane had the final say of the afternoon with a curling effort from the edge of the penalty area in the 76th minute to clinch our third place in the table. He became the first Spurs player to score 30 Premier League goals in a season and finished with an incredible 41 goals in all competitions.

141

v Fulham H (PL) - 18/8/18
77, right foot shot, inside area, W 3-1

Harry ended his August Premier League hoodoo with Spurs' third goal of the game after 77 minutes at Wembley. Erik Lamela laid the ball off to Kane in the area and he turned inside his marker before tucking a right-foot shot into the far corner.

142

v Manchester United A (PL) - 27/8/18
50, header, inside area, W3-0

Five minutes into the second half and Harry broke the deadlock to set Spurs on their way to a highly-impressive victory. Our striking talisman rose highest to meet a deep corner from Kieran Tripper and planted a powerful header back across goal and into the net.

143

v Brighton & Hove Albion A (PL)
- 22/9/18
42, penalty, W 2-1

Harry unleashed a thunderbolt penalty just three minutes before the break to open the scoring. After Glenn Murray had handled Kieran Trippier's free-kick, Kane emphatically beat Mathew Ryan with a trademark right-foot blast from 12 yards.

144

v Huddersfield Town A (PL)
- 29/9/18
25, header, inside area, W 2-0

145

v Huddersfield Town A (PL)
- 29/9/18
34, penalty, W 2-0

A first-half brace sealed another away win. Harry displayed all of his aerial prowess after 25 minutes when he rose at the back post to meet Kieran Trippier's tantalising cross and direct a firm header past Jonas Lossl. His second came from the penalty spot nine minutes later, lashing home a ferocious finish.

146

v Barcelona H (CL) - 3/10/18
52, right foot shot, inside area, L 4-2

Harry netted his first Champions League goal of 2018/19 seven minutes into the second half. Collecting the ball on the left, Kane carried the ball into the penalty area, shaped to shoot on his left but cut back onto his right to deceive Nelson Semedo before sending a curling effort into the far bottom corner.

147

v PSV Eindhoven A (CL) - 24/10/18
54, header, inside area, D 2-2

The second half in Holland was nine minutes old when Harry headed home Christian Eriksen's cross to put us 2-1 up. Lurking at the back post, Harry sent his header into the ground before the ball bounced up and into the roof of the net.

148

v Wolverhampton Wanderers A (PL) - 3/11/18
61, left foot shot, inside area, W 3-2

Despite a late comeback from the hosts, Harry's 61st minute goal proved to be the winner. Kane saw his initial shot repelled by the 'keeper before he hooked the loose ball home with his left foot.

149

v PSV Eindhoven H (CL) - 6/11/18
78, left foot shot, inside area, W 2-1

150

v PSV Eindhoven H (CL) - 6/11/18
89, header, inside area, W 2-1

Harry scored a brace in the final 12 minutes of this Champions League triumph at Wembley, to keep our hopes of progressing out of the group alive. His first came as he sent a first-time left-foot shot past 'keeper Jeroen Zoot. He then turned the match on its head in the 89th minute when his header from the edge of the six-yard box was deflected in. Harry's second took his Spurs tally to 150 as he became one of just five men to reach that milestone for the club.

151
v Chelsea H (PL) - 24/11/18
16, right foot shot, outside area, W 3-1

Harry ensured Spurs got off to a flying start at Wembley when he doubled our lead on 16 minutes. He pulled the trigger from 25 yards and his low well-struck effort left goalkeeper Kepa Arrizabalaga rooted to the spot as the ball flew in at the near post.

152
v Arsenal A (PL) - 2/12/18
34, penalty, L 4-2

Ultimately a day to forget for Spurs fans. However, it all looked so promising when Harry put us 2-1 ahead with a 34th-minute penalty, powerfully dispatching his spot-kick into the bottom left-hand corner following Rob Holding's foul on Heung-Min Son.

153
v Southampton H (PL) - 5/12/18
9, right foot shot, inside area, W 3-1

Once again it was one of Harry's perfectly timed runs to the near post that enabled him to open the scoring, arriving on cue to meet Christian Eriksen's whipped cross and steer a right-footed effort past Saints' goalkeeper Alex McCarthy.

154
v Everton A (PL) - 23/12/18
42, right foot shot, inside area, W 6-2

155
v Everton A (PL) - 23/12/18
74, right foot shot, inside area, W 6-2

Harry's first goal arrived three minutes before the break – after Kieran Trippier's excellent free-kick came back off the post, Kane reacted quickest to prod the loose ball into an empty net. His second came late on after he was fed the ball almost on the penalty spot by Heung-Min Son and he slotted past Jordan Pickford with a perfectly executed right-foot shot.

156
v Bournemouth H (PL) - 26/12/18
61, left foot shot, inside area, W 5-0

Harry netted our fifth goal of the game just after the hour when he sent a left-foot shot through the legs of visiting 'keeper Asmir Begovic, having been picked out by Christian Eriksen's perfectly weighted ball into the box.

157
v Wolverhampton Wanderers H (PL) - 29/12/18
22, left foot shot, outside area, L 3-1

Kane put Spurs in front with arguably one of his best goals. After collecting the ball in the right-hand channel he created a shooting angle for himself and let fly with a spectacular left-foot strike from 25 yards which beat goalkeeper Rui Patricio all ends up.

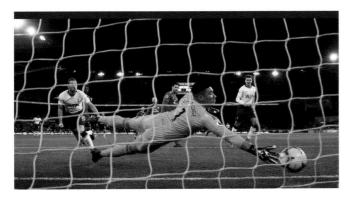

158
v Cardiff City A (PL) - 1/1/2019
3, right foot shot, inside area, W 3-0

It took our ace goal-getter just three minutes to make his mark in South Wales. Harry got our first goal of the game when he capitalised on Cardiff skipper Sean Morrison's haphazard clearance to score with a close-range right-foot finish.

159
v Tranmere Rovers A (FAC) - 4/1/2019
82, right foot shot, inside area, W 7-0

Despite starting on the bench, our number 10 came on as a substitute to score the seventh and final goal of this rout, taking Dele Alli's threaded pass in his stride before dinking the ball over the Rovers 'keeper with a cool finish.

160
v Chelsea H (LC) - 8/1/19
26, penalty, W 1-0

Kane moved past Cliff Jones to become Spurs' fourth highest goalscorer of all time, notching the only goal of this Carabao Cup semi-final, first leg tie. Kane left Kepa Arrizabalaga rooted to the spot with a precise penalty.

161
v Burnley A (PL) - 23/2/19
65, right foot shot, inside area, L 2-1

Harry returned from a period on the sidelines to score an excellent goal in this defeat. Straight from a Danny Rose long throw, Kane latched on to the ball and took on Burnley's defence before poking home accurately.

162

v Arsenal H (PL) - 2/3/19
74, penalty, D 1-1

In a tense north London derby at Wembley, Harry was on hand to convert from the spot to earn us a deserved draw, sending goalkeeper Bernd Leno the wrong way as his low spot-kick flew into the bottom left corner.

163

v Borussia Dortmund A (CL) - 5/3/19
48, right foot shot, inside area, W 1-0

Another record broken as Harry became our all-time top scorer in European competition, after scoring the only goal of the game. Leading 3-0 from the first leg, Kane exploited a hole in the Dortmund defence early in the second half, receiving Moussa Sissoko's through ball before hammering home to confirm our place in the quarter-finals.

164
v Southampton A (PL) - 9/3/19
26, right foot shot, inside area, L 2-1

Kane's final goal of the 2018/19 season was made by Dele Alli, who chipped a sumptuous ball through the Southampton defence. Harry took it in his stride, on the right of the penalty box before slotting the ball past goalkeeper Angus Gunn.

165
v Aston Villa H (PL) - 10/8/19
86, left foot shot, inside area, W 3-1

166
v Aston Villa H (PL) - 10/8/19
90, right foot shot, outside area, W 3-1

A great start to the 2019/20 season as Kane gets us up and running with a late double. He put us ahead on 86 minutes when he rammed home after the ball ricocheted nicely into his path, before adding another just before the final whistle, teeing himself up just outside the box before slotting home.

167

v Arsenal A (PL) - 1/9/19
40, penalty, D 2-2

Harry's goal in this match brought him level with Bobby Smith and Emmanuel Adebayor as the joint top scorers in the history of the north London derby. Christian Eriksen opened the scoring and we headed into the break two up after Kane slammed the ball into the bottom corner five minutes before the interval.

168

v Olympiacos A (CL) - 18/9/19
26, penalty, D 2-2

Harry opened the scoring in this Champions League match by firing a powerful penalty high into the centre of the net on 26 minutes. Lucas Moura scored four minutes later, but we would eventually have to settle for a point.

169

v Leicester City A (PL) - 21/9/19
29, right foot shot, inside area, L 2-1

Harry bagged a memorable goal in this defeat – best described as 'the one he scored while falling over'! Put through by Heung-Min Son, he barged between three Leicester defenders before starting to fall. He was set to land on the ball, so manoeuvred his body in a way that allowed his foot to send it flying into the top corner on his way down. Genius!

170

v Southampton H (PL) - 28/9/19
43, right foot shot, inside area, W 2-1

Harry scored our winner in a closely fought contest, finishing off a flowing move. Christian Eriksen nudged the ball to Kane inside the area, he took one touch to tee the ball up for himself and another to fire home on the half-volley into the bottom left corner.

171

v Bayern Munich H (CL) - 1/10/19
61, penalty, L 7-2

Kane was on hand to score on a difficult night up against the reigning Bundesliga champions. After Kingsley Coman fouled Danny Rose, we were awarded a penalty which Harry dispatched just after the hour mark, beating goalkeeper Manuel Neuer from the spot.

172

v Red Star H (CL) - 22/10/19
9, header, inside area, W 5-0

Nine minutes in, Harry made a darting run to the front post to meet an Erik Lamela corner, which he glanced home. He completed our rout when he made the most of a lovely pass from Tanguy Ndombele, venturing towards the left of the penalty box, drawing two defenders towards him, before threading a smart finish into the far corner.

173

v Red Star H (CL) - 22/10/19
72, right foot shot, inside area, W 5-0

QUOTE...
UNQUOTE

"We thought he had a good chance of becoming a good player. I'd watched him in training and in reserve games at the Training Centre and felt there was definitely a player there, but how good, nobody could tell. To beat Jimmy's record really is an amazing feat. He'll not only beat it, but smash it to pieces. He'll set a record that will never be beaten again."

— HARRY REDKNAPP

"Harry is a goal machine. He has no weakness – right foot, left foot, header – he's very dangerous in any position. There is no one player who deserves to break this record more than Harry."

HUGO LLORIS

"The best players for me are the ones that are multi-faceted in terms of their game. His all-round play is what makes him so difficult to play against and he can score all different types of goals. He's a complete footballer and that's what I love."

LEDLEY KING

"Dad's record was phenomenal, there is no-one else that has come near it but for Harry to break the record shows just what a good player and what a good goalscorer he is. That's what you have to be to break those kinds of records."

DANNY GREAVES (JIMMY'S SON)

"If you look at Harry's goalscoring record over the last decade, it's consistent and to have that consistency at the highest level is what separates the good players from the great players. There are a lot of players in football that can have a good two or three years but when you can keep doing it season after season, guaranteeing 20 plus goals every year, that puts you in a certain category. To have a player come through our Academy system and achieve what he's done in the game is pretty special. He's someone who is an inspiration to many."

RYAN MASON

"The best version of Harry Kane is unplayable, physically strong, mentally strong and just special. It's hard to find the words to describe what he's achieved with this record. To even be in the top 10 goalscorers, not just at any football club but at one of this size, with the players that have come before us like the legendary Jimmy Greaves, is special."

JERMAIN DEFOE

"You give the guy a chance and it tends to be a goal. I think he's the best finisher I've ever seen. He's the type of player that picks a team up when it's not doing so well. He's so professional, it's no coincidence that he's achieved what he has because of his work ethic. The hardest thing in football is to score goals, so if you are the best at it at your club then you have to go down as one of the greats."

BEN DAVIES

174

v Liverpool A (PL) - 27/10/19
1, header, inside area, L 2-1

We made the perfect start at Anfield when Harry scored inside 47 seconds. Heung-Min Son's shot deflected onto the crossbar via Joel Matip, and it landed into the lap of Kane who stooped to head into the corner beyond Alisson's reach.

175

v West Ham United A (PL) - 23/11/19
49, header, inside area, W 3-2

We raced into a 3-0 lead in this London derby when Serge Aurier's inch-perfect cross was converted by Kane with an excellent downward header past goalkeeper Lukasz Fabianski. West Ham rallied but we held on for a fully merited victory.

176

v Olympiacos H (CL) - 26/11/19
50, right foot shot, inside area, W 4-2

177

v Olympiacos H (CL) - 26/11/19
77, header, inside area, W 4-2

Harry's brace in this game saw him reach 20 Champions League goals faster than any player in the tournament's history (24 games). His first strike of the night arrived when Lucas Moura darted down the right flank and pulled back for Kane to tuck into the corner. Then Harry was on hand to score the final goal of the game on 77 minutes, rising highest to flick home from Christian Eriksen's free-kick.

178

v Burnley H (PL) - 7/12/19
5, right foot shot, outside area, W 5-0

179

v Burnley H (PL) - 7/12/19
54, right foot shot, inside area, W 5-0

Five minutes in, Harry approached the Clarets' penalty area and hammered home a piledriver from almost 30 yards and, in the second half, the Spurs striker jinked into the box, turned past James Tarkowski and fired into the top left corner. This was the day that Heung-Min Son scored an individual effort which would win the FIFA Puskas Award for Best Goal.

180

v Brighton & Hove Albion H (PL) - 26/12/19
53, right foot shot, inside area, W 2-1

Early in the second half of this Boxing Day win, Harry scored thanks to a mixture of poor defending and his own perseverance. The ball rebounded to him on the left of the area and, after Harry's initial shot was saved, he was alert enough to fire in an accurate angled volley on the follow-up.

181

v Norwich City A (PL) - 28/12/19
83, penalty, D 2-2

Spurs were staring defeat in the face until Harry's leveller at Carrow Road. Brought down in the penalty area by Christoph Zimmermann with less than 10 minutes remaining, Kane found the corner with the resulting spot-kick as he sent Tim Krul the wrong way.

182

v West Ham United H (PL) - 23/6/20
82, right foot shot, outside area, W 2-0

Another late strike, as Heung-Min Son spotted a gap in the Hammers' exposed backline and played a wonderful pass in to Kane, who ran at goalkeeper Lukasz Fabianski for what felt like an age, before calming slotting home.

183

v Sheffield United A (PL) - 2/7/20
90, right foot shot, inside area, L 3-1

Harry's 90th-minute goal at Bramall Lane – a right foot finish from close range after Heung-Min Son had squared from the left – proved to be nothing more than a consolation. The strike did at least keep up his record of scoring against every Premier League club he's faced.

184

v Newcastle United A (PL) - 15/7/20
60, header, inside area, W 3-1

185

v Newcastle United A (PL) - 15/7/20
90, header, inside area, W 3-1

Our number 10 was on the scoresheet twice at St. James' Park. His first was an excellent header back across goal from a Steven Bergwijn cross. Then, in the final minute of the match, he dived in bravely to head a rebound from an initial effort from Erik Lamela – that was palmed out by Magpies stopper Martin Dubravka – into the back of the net.

186

v Leicester City H (PL) - 19/7/20
37, left foot shot, inside area, W 3-0

187

v Leicester City H (PL) - 19/7/20
40, right foot shot, inside area, W 3-0

It was a case of 'Harry at the double' once again as Kane fired low past Kasper Schmeichel from Lucas Moura's pass on 37 minutes and cut in from the left wing before curling a superb finish into the corner for his second three minutes later.

188

v Crystal Palace A (PL) - 26/7/20
13, right foot shot, inside area, D 1-1

Harry netted at Selhurst Park despite there being plenty of bodies between him and the goal as he entered the box. His quick snap-shot caught Palace unawares as his effort arrowed precisely into the corner.

189

v Lokomotiv Plovdiv A (EL) - 17/9/20
80, penalty, W 2-1

This late equaliser was the spark that helped us come from behind to win this Europa League tie. It was a superb spot-kick in the 80th minute, rifled into the top left corner, which gave the goalkeeper absolutely no chance.

190

v Southampton A (PL) - 20/9/20
82, right foot, inside area, W 5-2

A magnificent performance from Kane saw him score once and make four assists – all for Heung-Min Son goals – at St Mary's. Harry got on the scoresheet late on after an Erik Lamela shot was pushed onto the post by Saints goalkeeper Alex McCarthy and our number 10 was on hand to slot the ball home.

191

v KF Shkendija A (EL) - 24/9/20
79, header, inside area, W 3-1

Harry met Heung-Min Son's out-swinging cross from the left to head comfortably across the goalkeeper into the back of the net in this Europa League play-off match.

192

v Maccabi Haifa H (EL) - 1/10/20
2, right foot shot, inside area, W 7-2

A 12th hat-trick for the Club and his first since December 2017 in a comprehensive victory. We were ahead within two minutes when Ben Davies squared onto the foot of Kane who had a tap in. Then in the second half, the skipper coolly slotted home a penalty before becoming the first Spur to hit three hat-tricks in Europe when Steven Bergwijn slipped him through and Harry dinked the ball over the goalkeeper.

193

v Maccabi Haifa H (EL) - 1/10/20
56, penalty, W 7-2

194

v Maccabi Haifa H (EL) - 1/10/20
74, left foot shot, inside area, W 7-2

195

v Manchester United A (PL) - 4/10/20

30, right foot shot, inside area, W 6-1

The first of two goals from Harry on a memorable afternoon at Old Trafford came on the half-hour mark as he finished first time from Heung-Min Son's pass across the United penalty area. He scored the game's final goal from the penalty spot on 79 minutes after Paul Pogba had brought down Ben Davies in the box.

196

v Manchester United A (PL) - 4/10/20

79, penalty, W 6-1

197

v West Ham United H (PL) - 18/10/20

8, right foot shot, outside area, D 3-3

198

v West Ham United H (PL) - 18/10/20

16, header, inside area, D 3-3

We were 3-0 up and cruising after 16 minutes of this London derby through a Heung-Min Son goal and a Kane brace. The England captain got his first of the day on eight minutes as he hit a shot from outside the penalty area beyond Lukasz Fabianski. He then headed Sergio Reguilon's inch-perfect cross back across the goalkeeper and into the unguarded net eight minutes later.

199

v Brighton & Hove Albion H (PL) - 01/11/20
13, penalty, W 2-1

Kane scored from the penalty spot on 13 minutes at Tottenham Hotspur Stadium. Seagulls stopper Robert Sanchez went to his right as Harry tucked the ball coolly into the opposite corner.

200

v Ludogorets A (EL) - 5/11/20
13, header, inside area, W 3-1

Harry became only the third player in our history to hit 200 goals for the Club when he netted after 13 minutes. On the occasion of his 300th Spurs appearance, he rose highest to head home from a Lucas Moura corner for the opener.

201

v West Bromwich Albion A (PL) - 8/11/20
88, header, inside area, W 1-0

The landmarks kept on coming as Harry scored the only goal of the game to bag his 150th Premier League strike. With two minutes remaining, Matt Doherty floated an inch-perfect ball into the box, and Kane lobbed goalkeeper Sam Johnstone with a delicate header.

202

v Arsenal H (PL) - 6/12/20
45+1, left foot shot, inside area, W 2-0

In first-half stoppage time, Harry scored the second of the game. Heung-Min Son tricked two defenders into thinking he was heading towards the right of the six-yard box before slipping in the overlapping Kane to his left. Harry produced a ruthless finish off the bar.

203
v Crystal Palace A (PL) - 13/12/20
23, right foot shot, outside area, D 1-1

Harry's shot from around 30 yards caught Palace's Vicente Guaita somewhat by surprise. Despite the Spanish goalkeeper getting his hands to the ball, the power and swerve deceived him and Kane's effort ended up in the back of the net.

204
v Stoke City A (LC) - 23/12/20
81, right foot shot, inside area, W 3-1

Progress to the semi-finals of the Carabao Cup was secured with Harry's late strike at the bet365 Stadium. Latching onto a Moussa Sissoko through ball, our number 10 held off his defender and then hammered a shot into the roof of the net.

205
v Leeds United H (PL) - 02/01/21
29, penalty, W 3-0

Harry was on target with a 29th-minute penalty in a comfortable win. He struck a firm spot-kick low and to the centre of the goal as goalkeeper Illan Meslier dived to his right.

206
v Fulham H (PL) - 13/01/21
25, header, inside area, D 1-1

Sergio Reguilon provided a sumptuous left-footed cross for Harry to head into the back of the net on 25 minutes, with his effort nicking the right post on its way in.

207
v Sheffield United A (PL) - 17/1/21
40, right foot shot, outside area, W 3-1

Kane saw off the close attention of a cluster of Sheffield United players to score at Bramall Lane, as he kept close control of the ball before hitting a low shot which crashed into the bottom right corner.

208

v West Bromwich Albion H (PL) - 7/2/21

54, right foot shot, inside area, W 2-0

Harry made it a seventh successive season of notching 20-plus goals when he netted after 54 minutes. Pierre-Emile Hojbjerg found Kane unmarked on the left of the penalty area and the England captain instinctively controlled and bent the ball delicately into the far corner.

209

v Everton A (FAC) - 10/2/21

83, header, inside area, L 5-4(aet)

Harry's strike at Goodison took him above Bobby Smith to become our second-highest goalscorer of all time. Heung-Min Son picked up his third assist of the match when his left-foot cross flashed high across the goalmouth and Harry met it at the back post, converting from close range with a diving header.

210

v Burnley H (PL) - 28/2/21
15, right foot shot, inside area, W 4-0

Kane added his name to the scoresheet with our second goal in a straightforward Premier League victory. The ace marksman latched on to Gareth Bale's long pass before dispatching a right foot shot past Clarets' goalkeeper Nick Pope.

211

v Crystal Palace H (PL) - 7/3/21
52, right foot shot, outside area, W 4-1

A second-half brace capped off a real man-of-the-match performance from Harry on an afternoon that also saw him provide two assists. His first goal came when he swept the ball past Vicente Guaita and into the far corner with an exceptional right-foot shot from outside the penalty area. Kane's second was another demonstration of the superb understanding that he has with strike partner Heung-Min Son as the South Korean teed up his teammate for a close-range header.

212

v Crystal Palace H (PL) - 7/3/21
76, header, inside area, W 4-1

213

v Dinamo Zagreb H (UEL) - 11/3/21
25, right foot shot, inside area, W 2-0

Another double for Harry, this time in Europe. After Erik Lamela hit the post, Harry was on to the loose ball in a flash and slid it into an unguarded net with his right foot to open the scoring. He doubled our advantage when the ball was pulled back to him in the penalty area and he cleverly worked it on to his right foot before driving the ball home.

214

v Dinamo Zagreb H (UEL) - 11/3/1
70, right foot shot, inside area, W 2-0

215

v Aston Villa A (PL) - 21/3/21
68, penalty, W 2-0

Harry rattled home his 17th Premier League goal of the campaign from the penalty spot, sending Villa goalkeeper Emiliano Martinez the wrong way by smashing the ball into the bottom left corner.

216

v Newcastle United A (PL) - 4/4/21
30, right foot shot, inside area, D 2-2

Kane scored twice in the first-half of an entertaining match at St James' Park. When Giovani Lo Celso slid a ball into the danger area after half an hour, Harry made the most of some hesitant defending from the home side to convert right footed from inside the six-yard box. His second goal arrived just four minutes later when he received the ball on the right edge of the area and took one touch to set himself before firing across goal and into the bottom corner.

217

v Newcastle United A (PL) - 4/4/21
34, right foot shot, inside area, D 2-2

218

v Everton A (PL) - 16/4/21
27, left foot shot, inside area, D 2-2

The magic figure of 20 Premier League goals for the season was reached when Kane made the most of time and space inside the penalty area to send a left-foot effort past Jordan Pickford. His next arrived when a mix-up in the Toffees' backline saw Erik Lamela's right-wing cross drop to Kane who rifled home a classic right-foot half-volley.

219

v Everton A (PL) - 16/4/21
68, right foot shot, inside area, D 2-2

220

v Wolverhampton Wanderers H (PL) - 16/5/21
45, right foot shot, inside area, W 2-0

Latching on to Pierre-Emile Hojbjerg's superb through ball, Harry opened the scoring despite the attention of opposing defenders, as he rounded goalkeeper Rui Patricio and slotted home with his trusty right foot.

221

v Leicester City A (PL) - 23/5/21
41, right foot shot, inside area, W 4-2

Volleying home a right-foot goal from inside the area on 41 minutes, Kane took his total in the Premier League to 23 for the season. That tally won him his third Golden Boot award having ended the campaign a goal ahead of Liverpool's Mo Salah and he also collected the Premier League's Playmaker award for most assists (14).

222

v Pacos de Ferreira H, (ECL) - 26/8/21
9, right foot shot, inside area, W 3-0

223

v Pacos de Ferreira H, (ECL) - 26/8/21
34, right foot shot, inside area, W3-0

A new season, but the same story as Harry was quickly among the goals. Picked out in the area by winger Bryan Gil, Kane took a touch and then stroked the ball into the bottom right-hand corner of the net with a right-foot finish. His second goal came after Giovani Lo Celso was crowded out in the area and the ball broke to Harry who calmly rolled it home from 12 yards.

224

v Wolverhampton Wanderers A (LC) - 22/9/21
23, right foot shot, inside area, D 2-2, W 3-2 on pens

After being played in by Dele Alli, Harry Kane sprinted clear of the Wolves defence and once in the penalty area he slotted a right-foot shot past the advancing John Ruddy.

225

v NS Mura H (ECL) - 30/9/21
68, right foot shot, inside area, W 5-1

Coming off the bench, Harry Kane netted an astonishing hat-trick inside 20 minutes and his treble made him the first Spurs player since Ronny Rosenthal in 1995 to score a hat-trick as a substitute. He grabbed his first after being played in by Lucas Moura and tucking home a firm right-foot effort before adding his second from Heung-Min Son's square ball. The treble was completed when Kane received a through ball from Giovani Lo Celso and fired home his 13th hat-trick for the club.

226

v NS Mura H (ECL) - 30/9/21
77, right foot shot, inside area, W 5-1

227

v NS Mura H (ECL) - 30/9/21
88, right foot shot, inside area, W 5-1

228

v Newcastle United A (PL) - 17/10/21
22, right foot shot, inside area, W 3-2

A first Premier League goal of the 2021/22 season for Harry arrived when he scored yet another goal on Tyneside. He bagged our second of the game with a right-foot lob over Karl Darlow having landed perfectly on Pierre-Emile Hojbjerg's precise through ball.

229

v NS Mura A (ECL) - 25/11/21
72, right foot shot, inside area, L 2-1

Kane netted his sixth goal in our 2021/22 Europa Conference League campaign when he scored after 72 minutes in Slovenia. Slipped in by Lucas Moura on the right side of the penalty area, Kane neatly lifted the ball over the advancing goalkeeper.

230

v Liverpool H (PL) - 19/12/21
13, right foot shot, inside area, D 2-2

Tottenham Hotspur Stadium witnessed Kane's first home Premier League goal of the season when he opened the scoring. His smart run into the Reds' box was spotted by Tanguy Ndombele and Harry neatly slotted a right-foot shot across goal and into the bottom corner.

231

v Crystal Palace H (PL) - 26/12/21
32, right foot shot, inside area, W 3-0

Harry put Spurs in front on 32 minutes, sweeping a first-time, right-foot shot beyond Jack Butland from Lucas Moura's pass. This goal equalled Robbie Fowler's Premier League record of nine goals scored on Boxing Day.

232

v Southampton A (PL) - 28/12/21
41, penalty, D 1-1

Harry signed off the calendar year of 2021 with a goal from the penalty spot. He beat current team-mate Fraser Forster when he drove his spot-kick home four minutes before half-time after Mohammed Salisu had fouled Heung-Min Son.

233

v Morecambe H (FA Cup) - 9/1/22
88, right foot shot, inside area, W 3-1

Picked out by Giovani Lo Celso with two minutes of the 90 remaining, with his back to goal Kane took an initial touch on the turn and then fired hard and low across the goal and into the bottom corner.

234

v Leicester City A (PL) - 19/1/22
38, left foot shot, inside area, W 3-2

A superb 250th career goal came in an eventful victory at Leicester City. Played in by Harry Winks on 38 minutes, Kane sprinted into the box and turned past defender Caglar Soyuncu before sending a crisp left-foot shot across goal which kissed the left-hand post on its way past Kasper Schmeichel.

235

v Brighton & Hove Albion H (FAC) - 5/2/22
13, right foot shot, outside area, W 3-1

Goals and records kept coming Harry's way as Spurs marched on in the FA Cup. He opened the scoring when he curled a right-foot beauty into the top corner from outside the area. His second arrived in the 66th minute when he prodded home from almost on the goal line having been the beneficiary of a great run from Heung-Min Son, a goal which took him to 300 for club and country.

236

v Brighton & Hove Albion H (FAC) - 5/2/22
66, right foot shot, inside area, W 3-1

237

v Manchester City A (PL) - 19/2/22
59, right foot shot, inside area, W 3-2

238

v Manchester City A (PL) - 19/2/22
90+5, header, inside area, W 3-2

Another brace in an outstanding individual performance as we completed a double over Premier League champions Manchester City. Harry's first came on 59 minutes when he converted a Heung-Min Son cross from the left before a dramatic winner five minutes into added time, out-jumping former Spurs team-mate Kyle Walker at the back post to head home Dejan Kulusevski's deep cross to spark scenes of wild celebration among the travelling fans behind the goal.

239

v Leeds United A (PL) - 26/2/22
27, left foot shot, inside area, W 4-0

Harry netted our third goal in a sensational first-half performance at Elland Road. Pierre-Emile Hojbjerg floated the ball to the back post where Kane had drifted in and lost his marker thus enabling him to instinctively hook home a left-foot finish from the tightest of angles.

240

v Everton H (PL) - 8/3/22
37, right foot shot, outside area, W 5-0

241

v Everton H (PL) - 8/3/22
55, left foot shot, inside area, W 5-0

Two goals against Everton took Harry to 20 goals in all competitions for the season. Sent through on goal from Matt Doherty's pass on 37 minutes, Kane took a touch to push the ball into his path before firing past Jordan Pickford with a low right-foot shot from the edge of the area. He bagged his second and our fifth after the break, Doherty again the provider with a hoisted ball to the back post where Kane struck with a brilliant angled left-foot volley.

242

v Manchester United A (PL) 12/3/22
35, penalty, L 3-2

Kane equalised from the penalty spot after Alex Telles had handled Dejan Kulusevski's cross. Harry kept his cool from 12 yards and despite David De Gea going the right way, the spot-kick was so accurately dispatched into the bottom left-hand corner that the United 'keeper had no chance.

243

v Brighton & Hove Albion A (PL) - 16/3/22
57, left foot shot, inside area, W 2-0

Harry became the Premier League's all-time top scorer of away goals in this win on the south coast. Latching on to a Rodrigo Bentancur pass, he sent a low left-foot effort past Robert Sanchez to give him 95 Premier League goals on the road, surpassing Wayne Rooney's previous record.

244

v Leicester City H (PL) - 1/5/22
22, header, inside area, W 3-1

Quickly peeling away from his marker and into space, Kane met Heung-Min Son's corner with a firm header from the edge of the six-yard box. As the ball flew past Kasper Schmeichel at his near post, this was Harry's 18th goal against the Foxes in 18 appearances.

245

v Arsenal H (PL) - 12/5/22
22, penalty, W 3-0

246

v Arsenal H (PL) - 12/5/22
37, header, inside area, W 3-0

Always the man for the big occasion, Harry delivered another North London derby double as Spurs cruised to a vital victory in the race for the top four. He opened the scoring when he drove a penalty hard and low into the bottom right-hand corner after Cedric Soares had fouled Heung-Min Son. His second came when Rodrigo Bentancur flicked on a corner towards goal and Harry stooped low to head home from close range at the back post.

247

v Burnley H (PL) - 15/5/22
45+8, penalty, W 1-0

On the stroke of half-time, Kane converted his second penalty of the week at Tottenham Hotspur Stadium. Awarded after a lengthy VAR review for a handball by Ashley Barnes, Harry maintained his composure and sent a precise right-foot spot-kick low into the left-hand corner.

248

v Norwich City A (PL) - 22/5/22
32, header, inside area, W 5-0

On an afternoon when strike partner Heung-Min Son bagged a brace and won the 2021/22 Golden Boot award, Harry was among the goals too as Spurs secured fourth place. Rodrigo Bentancur capitalised on a poor clearance from Norwich goalkeeper Tim Krul and crossed for the right for Harry to head home after 32 minutes.

249

v Chelsea A (PL) - 14/8/22
90+6, header, inside area, D 2-2

Harry opened his scoring account for 2022/23 when he headed in a last-gasp equaliser against Chelsea. Six minutes into added time at Stamford Bridge, Harry climbed highest in the Blues' penalty area to powerfully head home Ivan Perisic's corner.

250

v Wolverhampton Wanderers H (PL) - 21/8/22

64, header, inside area, W 1-0

Harry bagged his 250th goal in our colours when he headed home our 64th-minute winner. Heung-Min Son's corner was flicked on at the near post by Ivan Perisic and Kane headed home his landmark goal at the back post. It was a significant one for the Club – our 1,000th at home in the Premier League.

251

v Nottingham Forest A (PL) - 28/8/22

5, right foot shot, edge of box, W 2-0

A quality counter-attacking move saw us ahead early at the City Ground, as Dejan Kulusevski pick out Harry on the right-hand edge of the penalty area and he sent a crisp shot past goalkeeper Dean Henderson. He added his second goal of the game nine minutes from time when Richarlison crossed from the left and Harry planted a firm header home from close range.

252

v Nottingham Forest A (PL) - 28/8/22

81, header, inside area, W 2-0

253

v Fulham H (PL) - 4/9/22
75, left foot shot, inside area, W 2-1

Kane bagged our second goal of the game on 75 minutes after an effort from Ryan Sessegnon ran loose off the hand of Fulham goalkeeper Bernd Leno and our number 10 swept home a left-foot shot from close range.

254

v Leicester City H (PL) - 17/9/22
8, header, inside area, W 6-2

Harry's phenomenal goalscoring record against Leicester continued as he headed home after eight minutes. Dejan Kulusevski sent a deep cross towards the back post and there was Harry to take his tally to 19 against the Foxes.

255
v Arsenal A (PL) - 1/10/22
31, penalty, L 3-1

A north London derby goal from the penalty spot took Kane's scoring record against the Gunners to 14. Harry banged his spot-kick straight down the middle to beat Aaron Ramsdale on 31 minutes after defender Gabriel had upended Richarlison. He became the first player to score 100 Premier League away goals with this strike.

256
v Brighton & Hove Albion (A) - PL - 8/10/22
22, header, inside area, W 1-0

Midway through the first half, Kane scored with an instinctive header. Heung-Min Son collected Pierre-Emile Hojbjerg's pass from a cleared corner and whipped in a driven cross which Kane flicked into the net from six yards out.

257
v Eintracht Frankfurt H (CL) - 12/10/22
28, penalty, W 3-2

Harry thumped home a 28th-minute Champions League penalty to put us in front having been bundled over in the box by Kristijan Jakic. The spot-kick was perfectly dispatched into the right-hand side of the net leaving goalkeeper Kevin Trapp helpless.

258
v Everton H (PL) - 15/10/22
59, penalty, W 2-0

A 400th appearance for Spurs was marked with the opening goal of the game at Tottenham Hotspur Stadium. Harry himself had been fouled by Jordan Pickford for the resulting penalty which he then fired past the goalkeeper and into the left-hand side of the goal.

259
v Newcastle United H (PL) - 23/10/22
54, header, inside area, L 2-1

A second-half header reduced the arrears as Kane reached double figures for the season in the Premier League once again. Nine minutes into the second half and Heung-Min Son's corner was flicked on by Clement Lenglet to Kane who bravely stooped at the back post to head home.

260
v Liverpool H (PL) - 06/11/22
70, right foot shot, inside area, L 2-1

A well-worked goal saw Matt Doherty and Dejan Kulusevski involved in the build-up before the Swede played a delightful pass into the path of Harry, who received the ball on the angle of the six-yard box and sent a low first-time right-foot shot across goal and into the bottom corner.

261
v Leeds United H (PL) - 12/11/22
25, right foot shot, inside area, W 4-3

After Leeds goalkeeper Illan Meslier punched a 25th-minute corner clear, Harry seized upon the loose ball, producing a wonderful touch to see off the attentions of marker Tyler Adams before hammering a right-footed shot into the corner.

262
v Brentford A (PL) - 26/12/22
65, header, inside area, D 2-2

Harry was on the scoresheet as we came from two goals down to get a point at the Brentford Community Stadium. On 65 minutes, Clement Lenglet swung a sumptuous left-footed cross into the Bees penalty and our number 10 rose majestically to put a powerful header in the far corner.

263
v Crystal Palace A (PL) - 04/01/23
48, header, inside area, W 4-0

264
v Crystal Palace A (PL) - 04/01/23
53, right foot shot, inside area, W 4-0

Three minutes after the interval, Harry showed great desire to score our opening goal at Selhurst Park, leaping high at the back post to head home from Ivan Perisic's cross. He doubled our advantage on 53 minutes with a low, right-footed shot from a tight angle, as Bryan Gil claimed the assist.

265
v Portsmouth H (FA Cup) - 07/01/23
50, right foot shot, outside area, W 1-0

A curling, right-footed shot from the edge of the penalty area from Kane saw us book our place in the fourth round of FA Cup. Collecting the ball just outside the 18-yard-box, Kane played a one-two with Ryan Sessegnon then took a touch to set himself before unleashing an unstoppable effort beyond Portsmouth goalkeeper Josh Griffiths.

266

v Fulham A (PL) - 23/1/12
45, right foot shot, outside area, W 1-0

A landmark goal on his 300th Premier League appearance for Spurs, as Harry netted his 266th goal in our colours to draw level with Jimmy Greaves. On a bitterly cold night in west London, Kane warmed the hearts of Spurs fans everywhere with the winner in first-half stoppage time. Heung-Min Son played the ball into Harry, back to goal on the edge of the area and, with one quick touch to his left, he worked a yard of space to be able to curl right-footed past an unsighted Bernd Leno, the ball kissing the far post on its way in.

"Once Sonny got the ball, I tried to get myself in a position where I could get half a yard so I could get my shot away. I used the defender to just bend it round him into the far corner and it's hard for the keeper then because he's unsighted. It was a nice goal, a nice way to bring me level with Greavsie."

HARRY KANE

MY TOP 5

267

v Manchester City H (PL) - 5/2/23
15, right foot shot, inside area, W 1-0

Spurs fans will always remember where they were on 5 February 2023 – the day Tottenham Hotspur history was re-written. Harry had been edging closer to the magical figure of 267 goals since returning from World Cup duty with England in December and it finally arrived on the big stage – against reigning champions Manchester City at Tottenham Hotspur Stadium.

In his interview in this magazine, Harry mentions his classic style of goal is a right-foot finish across the goalkeeper and into the bottom corner, so it was fitting that he produced exactly that to break the record!

Pierre-Emile Hojbjerg stole possession deep inside the City half and found Kane inside the area, allowing him to provide the record-breaking moment everyone had been waiting for. The goal was met with a tremendous roar from the crowd inside the stadium, who knew they were watching history unfold in front of their eyes and Harry himself was emotional when he addressed the fans on the pitch after the game. "I wanted to break the record somewhere special and there's no better place to do it than here in front of these amazing fans," he said.

Goal number 267 in the bag. History made. One of our own.

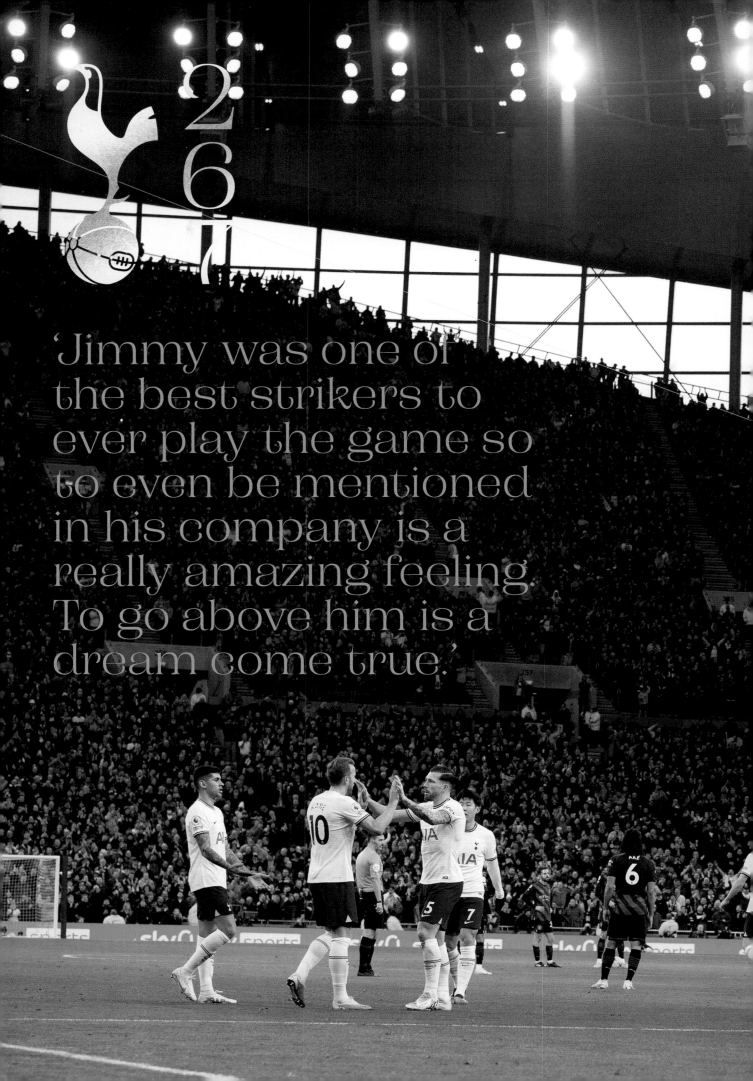

2
6

'Jimmy was one of
the best strikers to
ever play the game so
to even be mentioned
in his company is a
really amazing feeling
To go above him is a
dream come true.'